Darwin and Evolution *for* Kids

Darwin and Evolution *for* Kids

HIS LIFE AND IDEAS
with 21 Activities

Kristan Lawson

CHICAGO
REVIEW
PRESS

Library of Congress Cataloging-in-Publication Data
Lawson, Kristan.
Darwin and evolution for kids : his life and ideas,
with 21 activities / by Kristan Lawson.— 1st ed.
        p.   cm.
Summary: A biography of the English naturalist
who, after collecting plants and animals from
around the world, postulated the theory of evolution by natural selection. Includes related activities. Includes bibliographical references and
index.
    ISBN 1-55652-502-8
1. Darwin, Charles, 1809–1882—Juvenile literature.
2. Naturalists—England—Biography—Juvenile literature. 3. Evolution (Biology)—Study and teaching—Activity programs. [1. Darwin, Charles,
1809–1882. 2. Naturalists. 3. Scientists. 4. Evolution (Biology)] I. Title.
    QH31.D2L39 2003
    576.8'2'092—dc21   2003007473

Front cover photos: Blue-footed boobies, © Digital Vision/Wonderfile;
Darwin portrait © North Wind Picture Archives
Photo credits: Pages 128, 136, and 137 courtesy of the W. C. Robinson and
Sue K. Hall Collections, Special Collections, University of Tennessee, Knoxville

Cover and interior design: Laura Lindgren Design
Activity illustrations: Laura D'Argo and Anneli Rufus

Published by Chicago Review Press, Incorporated
814 North Franklin Street
Chicago, Illinois 60610
ISBN 1-55652-502-8
Printed in the United States of America
5 4 3 2 1

Note to Readers

If you can't wait to learn about evolution, a clear explanation of Darwin's theory can be found in Chapter 6. Readers mostly interested in learning about evolution (instead of Darwin's life story) are encouraged to skip ahead and read Chapter 6 first. More information about the development and growth of the theory can be found in the other chapters.

Acknowledgments

Thanks to Jerome Pohlen and Anneli Rufus for their help.

Contents

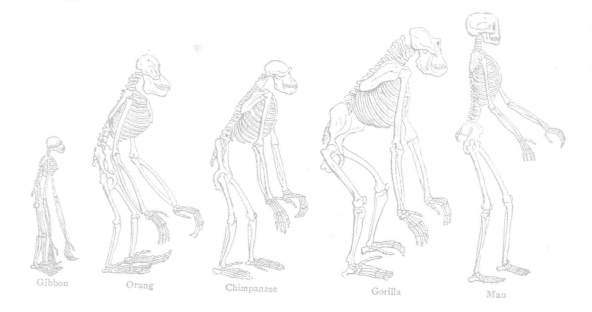

Gibbon   Orang   Chimpanzee   Gorilla   Man

Time Line

1654 — Bishop James Ussher calculates that the Earth was created on October 23, 4004 B.C.

1735 — Linnaeus devises the system for classifying all types of animals that is still used to this day

1798 — Thomas Malthus writes his *Essay on the Principle of Population*

1809 — Charles Darwin is born in Shrewsbury, England

1825 — Darwin is taken out of school due to poor performance, and sent to Edinburgh to study medicine

1827 — Darwin quits medical school and transfers to Cambridge, where he studies to become a clergyman

1831 — Darwin begins an around-the-world voyage on the HMS *Beagle*

1832 — Darwin explores the jungles of Brazil and the coast of Argentina, collecting thousands of plants, animals, and fossils

1835 — The *Beagle* visits the Galapagos Islands

1836 — The *Beagle* arrives back in England after nearly five years at sea

1838 — Darwin begins a secret notebook all about evolution, or "the transmutation of species," as he called it

Darwin reads Malthus's *Essay on the Principle of Population* and formulates the theory of natural selection

1839 — Darwin marries his cousin, Emma Wedgwood

Darwin's first book, about his voyage on the *Beagle,* is published

1842 — Darwin writes the first rough draft of his theory of evolution

Darwin's family moves to Down House, Kent

1846	Darwin becomes fascinated by barnacles, and spends the next eight years studying them
1854	Darwin publishes a series of books about barnacles
1858	Darwin receives a paper from Alfred Russel Wallace describing a theory of natural selection that exactly matches Darwin's own
1859	Darwin writes and publishes *On the Origin of Species,* which instantly makes him world-famous
1863	A newly discovered lizard-bird fossil called Archaeopteryx seems to confirm Darwin's theory
1865	Gregor Mendel publishes the results of his experiments on heredity
1871	*The Descent of Man,* Darwin's second most famous book, is published
1872	Darwin publishes *The Expression of the Emotions in Man and Animals*
1875	Darwin publishes *Insectivorous Plants*
1882	Charles Darwin dies on April 19, and is buried in Westminster Abbey
1900	Mendel's experiments are rediscovered, launching the field of genetics
1925	John Scopes, during the famous "Monkey Trial," is convicted of teaching evolution
1953	The structure of DNA as the basis for heredity is discovered

Introduction

Charles Darwin was tired. For two years, ever since he had returned to England from his around-the-world voyage aboard the HMS *Beagle,* he had been writing about the animals, plants, and fossils he had collected while traveling. When the ship had finally arrived home in October 1836, the young man was relieved to be back after five years at sea. His living conditions on the small *Beagle* had been cramped and uncomfortable, and he had often been very seasick. But during his travels he had found thousands of strange and exotic animals, rare plants, and mysterious fossils. He was eager to write a book about all his new discoveries.

Darwin's homecoming filled him with energy. Having grown up in the English countryside, he now moved to London for the first time in his life. There, the young naturalist rented a room and set to work on what he hoped would be his great masterpiece.

But after two years of writing, his one book had grown into three separate books, and only one of them was done. The task seemed unending. He found that he couldn't concentrate on only one topic. As he pored over each specimen, his mind started to ponder bigger questions: Where had all the different animals in the world come from? And why did fossils always look different from living creatures?

To make matters worse, Darwin realized that he hated living in the big city. He loved the wide-open spaces of his childhood and of the wild lands he had visited on his voyage. Now, when he looked out his window, all he could see were London's grimy streets, polluted air, and bustling crowds. He needed to take a break, to clear his head.

So in 1838 he started reading a few books for fun—whatever interesting titles caught his eye. Anything to get his mind off the boxes of specimens

Almost everyone in Darwin's era believed that God had created all life and that no new creatures had appeared since the first days of creation.

and scribbled notes stacked up all around his room!

On that evening in late October, while relaxing in his study, he picked up a copy of a book called *Essay on the Principle of Population,* which had been written 40 years earlier but which was still a best-seller. The author was a minister named Thomas Malthus, who had tried to figure out why there were always so many poor people in England. Even though the book wasn't as entertaining as an adventure story or a romance novel, Darwin was glad to be reading something that had nothing whatsoever to do with his own work on plants and animals.

Or so he thought. It turns out Darwin couldn't have been more mistaken.

✳

During his worldwide voyage, Darwin had learned what other scientists already knew: that there were many more kinds of animals in the world than people in the past had ever imagined. In ancient times, when the story of Noah's Ark was written, people thought that there were at most a hundred different kinds of animals—dogs, cats, cows, lions, mice, sheep, foxes, hawks, sparrows, beetles, deer, monkeys, and so on; quite a variety but few enough that Noah could easily fit them all into his ark. But by Darwin's time in the mid-1800s, explorers had discovered thousands and thousands of different kinds of animals, and every year hundreds more were being added to the list. As Darwin looked over his specimens, he often wondered: Had each species appeared fully formed, separate from every other

species? Or were they somehow all related to each other? What especially intrigued Darwin was how certain species were very similar to each other, but still a little different in notable ways. This kind of bird had a slightly longer beak than that kind; this kind of monkey looked just like that kind of monkey except that it had sharper teeth. Why?

Darwin was becoming convinced that millions of years ago all animals had started from a single ancestor, but that little by little the creatures changed until eventually several different types appeared. These types developed into all the animals we see today. The name later given to this process was *evolution.* The idea had been around for a long time, but what no one—including Darwin—had ever been able to figure out was *how* animals evolved. Many ideas were suggested over the years, but they all seemed unlikely. One respected writer even declared that animals grew new features through sheer willpower! The more Darwin tried to concentrate on his specimens, the more his thoughts drifted to what he called "the species question." In fact, Darwin was so interested in this topic that he had started a secret notebook to record his thoughts on evolution while he wrote about his *Beagle* adventure.

But that fall evening in 1838, as he picked up Malthus's book, evolution was the last thing on his mind. He just wanted to relax. So he sat back with a sigh and started to read.

The main point Malthus tried to make in his book was that there were just too many people in the world. He stated that the planet's population

It was a struggle just to survive in the overcrowded cities of England.

was growing faster than humankind's ability to grow enough food to feed everyone. Because of this, people were always fighting in order to get enough to eat and struggling amongst themselves to have the most comfortable lives. In this struggle, some were winners and, unfortunately, some were losers. Those who came out on the losing side ended up begging on the streets and living in the crowded slums of cities like London. Every now and then, Malthus pointed out, when the size of the population got out of hand, some kind of disaster inevitably came along to kill off its weakest members. Sometimes this disaster was a famine; other times it was a plague, a war, or some other catastrophe. But, according to Malthus, the root cause of poverty and suffering was the tendency of the human race to increase its population far more quickly than it could be fed.

All this seemed sensible to Darwin. But then he realized that the same principles are true for *all* animal species, not just humans. In the wild, most types of animals give birth to large litters, yet most of these baby animals never grow up because they either starve to death or are eaten by predators.

Of course! Why had it never occurred to him before? The idea that struck Darwin at that moment was so amazing yet so obvious that he practically dropped the book on the floor. Malthus had unknowingly revealed to him the secret of evolution that had mystified scientists for generations.

Darwin's own observations in nature had shown him that animals usually gave birth to far more babies than could ever survive. So, he wondered, what was so special about those few that managed to stay alive? Darwin knew that every living thing was slightly different from all its brothers and sisters. If a baby rabbit, for example, had weaker legs than its sister, it would be less able to run away from a fox. So the fox would catch and eat the slower rabbit, while its faster sister would run away and survive, and eventually grow up and give birth to babies of her own. These baby rabbits would inherit strong, fast legs from their mother. And then the process would repeat itself when those babies grew up and had *their* babies. In this way, little by little, a species would change with every generation—developing better muscles for running, different-colored fur for camouflage, longer necks for reaching food, and so on. With enough time and enough generations, it was possible that every single species on Earth had evolved this way.

In 1838 this was a shocking idea. Most people believed that God had created the whole world and its creatures in only six days, just as it said in the Bible. Darwin was afraid that people would laugh at him or attack him if he revealed his theory. So he kept his brilliant idea to himself, writing it down in his secret notebook. Little did he know that this "secret" notebook would grow and grow for 20 years. Nor did he know that one day it would be published and hailed as one of the greatest books ever written.

Before Darwin

This is not just the story of a man. It's also the story of an idea that changed the world.

Charles Darwin is as unlikely a hero as you'll ever meet. He spent almost half his life sick in bed—or at least pretending to be sick. He was a bad student and barely made it through school. He authored several famous books but found writing a painful chore and struggled to express himself with words. He had terrible stage fright and couldn't defend his work in public. Though he sailed around the world, he would immediately get seasick whenever he stepped onto a boat. Despite being considered one of the greatest thinkers who ever lived, he was unable to control his own thoughts or emotions: he drove himself to distraction obsessing over unimportant details, and was often in a foul mood. He was filled with fear—of disease, of dying, and, worst of all, of rejection.

What a strange man! Why is he so famous? Underneath all these personality quirks was a reluctant genius. Although he didn't realize it, his whole life was spent creating and polishing one of the most important ideas in history. Nowadays, we use a single word to sum up this earth-shattering concept: *evolution*. But amazingly, Darwin himself never used this term to describe his theory. He preferred the more accurate (though harder to remember) phrase *transmutation through natural selection*. Yet even this term (which will be defined later) fails to convey the universe of ideas hidden within it.

Darwin was trying to explain where all the animals and plants in the world had come from. But in so doing he accidentally revealed one of the underlying principles of the universe. Evolution, it turned out, was not just about animals; it happens all around us, every day. We've slowly come to realize that almost *everything* evolves: languages,

Scientists in Darwin's era were the first to wonder what the Earth looked like millions of years ago.

galaxies, fashions, ecosystems, ideas, relationships, diseases, cultures, and much more. Even the theory of evolution has itself evolved! Yet Darwin could never have predicted how far-reaching his ideas would someday turn out to be. He was only trying to figure out why the birds he saw on an obscure group of islands had different-sized beaks.

Evolution Before Darwin

Charles Darwin was not the first person to discover the concept of evolution. It had been around for centuries. He did not even invent the principle of natural selection. Darwin's unique achievement was to be the first person who brought these two ideas together into a single theory and to present overwhelming evidence of its truth.

Before Darwin, the vast majority of people in the world never gave a thought to the origin of animal species. They assumed that animals had looked and acted the same way forever. A cat was a cat, a pig was a pig. It was common sense. After all, no one had ever *seen* one kind of animal changing into another. Besides, the Bible says that God created all the animals long ago, and most people believed the Bible is always right. But as far back as ancient Greece, deep-thinking philosophers had speculated that evolution—or the changing of one species into another—*must* occur. What no one before Darwin had ever figured out was *how* it occurred.

Around 450 B.C. a Greek philosopher named Empedocles wrote that animals of every type had

evolved from plants, but that most of them never survived. If they had features that did not enable them to eat and reproduce, then they would naturally die out. That is why, he reasoned, we only see well-adapted animals; the ill-adapted animals all went extinct. Amazingly, this idea from ancient times was very close to the concept of natural selection that Darwin developed 2,300 years later. Unfortunately, few people ever learned of Empedocles' ideas.

Aristotle, the famous Greek philosopher from the fourth century B.C., believed that certain types of animals were more advanced than others. He was the first person to create a taxonomy, or classification of life forms. He taught that all of life could be organized into a "Ladder of Creation." Bugs and snakes were the lowest because they crawled on the ground. Humankind was the highest because of its powerful minds. This way of looking at the world was very influential, and in Darwin's era most people agreed with Aristotle that human beings were "more advanced" or better than the "lower animals."

Many other ancient philosophers, such as Democritus and Anaximander, also promoted evolutionary ideas in their writings. They believed the world and everything in it had slowly evolved from nothingness and was constantly changing.

This period of intellectual freedom was not to last. During the Dark Ages and Middle Ages in Europe (about 400–1400 A.D.), the Catholic Church reigned supreme, and belief in the literal truth of the Bible was enforced by law. Evolutionary thinking disappeared entirely. The ancient philosophers were

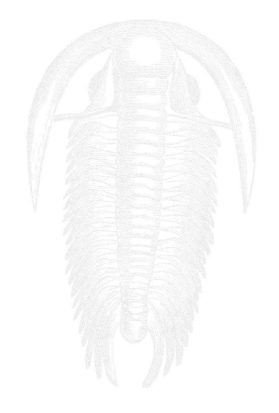

forgotten. The common belief was that God had created all animals on the fifth and sixth days of Creation, as described in the Book of Genesis. After that, God's job was done, and nothing new has ever come into the world. Therefore, all types of animals have existed since the beginning of time. Any other belief was considered heresy, a crime punishable by death.

In the Middle Ages, horrific punishments awaited those who dared to contradict the Bible.

Taxonomy

Taxonomy is the science of classifying things into related families and groups. The Swedish naturalist Carolus Linneaus created a taxonomy for all animals and plants that was so well organized that scientists still use it today. But you can design a creative taxonomy of your own that includes any type of object at all.

What you need
20–50 different small objects
20–50 slips of heavy paper or card stock
a very large piece of paper
transparent tape

For the slips of heavy paper, you can use the blank sides of old business cards, or heavy construction paper cut into 2-inch (5-cm) squares—even a cut-up old cereal box. For the very large piece of paper, you can use the back side of an old poster, or a piece of butcher paper, or the blank side of a piece of wrapping paper.

Wander around your backyard, your neighborhood, and your house collecting a wide variety of interesting and varied small objects: twigs, dead bugs, small toys, parts of plants, rocks, nuts, hair ornaments, game pieces, erasers, shells—whatever you find!

Spread everything out on the floor. Pick up one object and write what the object is in capital letters across the top of one card. Then write down on the card the object's basic attributes according to any of several categories. You can make up whatever categories you like, but here are some you can use and choose from:

Material it is made out of? *(Plastic, wood, metal, animal material, etc.)*
Organic or inorganic? *(Organic refers to anything that was once alive, or part of something that was alive. For example, a leaf is organic, because it was once part of a tree, as is anything made out of wood, like a toothpick. A rock, or something made out of metal, is inorganic, because it was never alive.)*
Color? *(Green, brown, red, multicolored, etc.)*
Was it found inside or outside?
Irregularly shaped, or symmetrical?
Edible or not edible?
Sinks in water, or floats in water?
Does it have legs?

If you used these categories, for example, the card for a small broken pencil that you found under the couch might look like this:

PENCIL
Wood
Organic
Yellow
Inside
Symmetrical
Not edible
Floats
No legs

Make a card for each object. Try to use the same categories on every card. If you are unsure about any aspect of any object, ask someone who might know. Sometimes the answer might surprise you! (For example, an eraser is organic because it is made of rubber, which comes from rubber trees.) When you're done making the cards, spread them out on the large piece of paper and write across the top, in large letters, "Taxonomy Chart."

Now for the really creative part. Start arranging the cards on the large piece of paper into groupings that make sense to you. Put the cards for all the plastic things together, and for all red things in a different group, and for all the edible things somewhere else. But what if you have a red plastic button? Arrange all the plastic thing cards in a group, and have the button card slightly below them, and right next to the button card put all the red things. This shows that the button is part of both groups. Keep doing this and rearranging cards until you're satisfied that they are arranged in the best possible way, so that similar categories and objects are near each other. A good way to start is to divide all objects into two major groups (such as "Inside" and "Outside") and then subdivide those groups into smaller categories, and so on.

Once you're completely satisfied with your arrangement, tape all the cards down in place. Then, draw lines (it's helpful to use a ruler) connecting all the groups of objects in a way that shows the relationships between them. If you want to, write identifying terms above each group.

When you're done, tape your chart to the wall.

The Rise of Science

During the Renaissance and the Age of Enlightenment (15th–18th centuries), people become more open-minded and the Catholic Church gradually became less influential. Scientific discoveries—such as the fact that the Earth revolved around the sun—showed that the Bible isn't always literally true. So, at this time, people began to regard the Bible mostly as a moral guide instead of a source of historical or scientific information. The change in the intellectual climate was slow and gradual, however. In England, the Anglican Church was still very conservative.

Many scientists tried to present their discoveries in a way that wouldn't offend the church. The concept of "Special Creation" was one attempt to merge new discoveries with church doctrine. Throughout the 17th and 18th centuries, more and more animals, plants, and fossils were being discovered by explorers all over the world. People began to wonder: Did God really create these thousands of species all across the globe all at the same time? What about the fossil record? New animals appear in certain layers, and old ones disappear. Where did they come from if God didn't make them on the fifth and sixth days of Creation?

Jean Baptiste Lamarck.

The answer was a compromise called *Special Creation.* Each new species was indeed created by God, but not necessarily at the beginning of time. Every now and then, according to this approach, God created new animals and plants in acts of "Special Creation" that took place *after* the incidents described in the Book of Genesis. This would explain the origins of species that seem to have appeared fairly recently. But once species are created, people said, they always stay the same, the way God made them.

The doctrine of Special Creation satisfied nearly everyone. The explorers, natural historians, pale-ontologists, and scientists could continue their advances without worrying that some new discovery would contradict Christian belief. And the church was happy to confirm that everything on Earth was still indeed created directly by God.

By the late 1700s, a new push for evolution emerged, however. The leading proponents were Erasmus Darwin (Charles's grandfather) and Jean Baptiste Lamarck. They both proposed a concept now known as "the inheritance of acquired characteristics." Lamarck, who was a professor of zoology at the Museum of Natural History in Paris, knew more about animals than almost anyone in the world at the time. Noticing the many striking similarities between species, he became convinced that they were related to each other, and that evolution was the only way to explain the connections. He was right about that. Yet he was unsure what caused evolution. Like Erasmus Darwin, he proposed that animals changed their forms either through willpower or through being influenced by the environment. Then when these altered animals had offspring, their babies inherited these new characteristics. Lamarck gave a famous example: a giraffe would stretch its neck to reach the tastiest leaves at the top of a tree. After a while its neck would grow longer. Then when it gave birth to baby giraffes, they too would inherit longer necks from their mother. (Try the "Acquired Characteristics" activity in Chapter 2 to see if he was right or not!)

The problem with this theory is that no one had ever seen it happen, and there was no evidence it ever occurred in nature. There *was* evidence against

Lamarck wondered whether giraffes had evolved long necks by stretching to reach the tops of trees.

it. Critics pointed out that blacksmiths, who had developed strong arm muscles from pounding iron, still fathered children with normal-sized arms, like those of any average baby. A woman who had a finger chopped off would still give birth to a child with 10 fingers. As far as anyone could tell, characteristics acquired during people's lifetimes were *not* passed on to their offspring.

A Divine Watchmaker

Another blow to evolution arrived in 1802. An influential clergyman named William Paley published an interesting argument: If you were to find a stone on the ground and someone asked you, "Where did that stone come from?" you might answer, "It's probably been here forever." But if you were to find a *watch* on the ground, and someone asked you the same question, you'd have to stop and think. The watch has hundreds of tiny gears and springs and dials, and is so finely made that it couldn't have just appeared randomly on the ground or somehow magically assembled itself out of natural materials. The watch was obviously designed and made by someone—a watchmaker, presumably. Now, Reverend Paley went on to argue, look at all the animals of the world. They are much more complicated than a watch. Wings and veins and brains and muscles and cells and bones, all working together in perfect harmony. It seems impossible that such a thing might arise by chance, at random, without a plan. If the existence of a watch implied the existence of a designer, Paley said, then something more complicated than a watch—the anatomy of any animal—implied the existence of a designer even more. As Paley put it, "Design must have had a designer. That designer must have been a person. That person is God." In other words, something as random and purposeless and unintelligent as nature could never have accidentally created something as intricate and interconnected and "perfect" as a living body—especially a human being.

Many were convinced by Paley's argument. It just didn't seem possible that evolution (i.e., the blind forces of nature) could have led to the immensely complicated life-forms all around us.

And this is about how things stood when Charles Darwin was born in 1809. The argument over evolution continued, but the people who believed in Creation (or Special Creation) and in Paley's "Divine Watchmaker" theory had the upper hand. Why? Because no one had yet come up with a convincing explanation for *how* evolution occurred. Until the evolutionists could discover what principle caused species to change, evolution would remain pure speculation. The idea was interesting to a few, funny to some. But to most people it was a dangerous notion that contradicted the Bible. Evolution still faced a tough road ahead.

Darwin's England

Charles Darwin was born in 1809 and died 73 years later, in 1882. The era in which he lived—19th-century England—was quite different from the modern world.

Explorers noticed that the okapi looked just like a giraffe with a short neck. Could giraffes and okapis be related?

Most of the inventions now taken for granted did not yet exist. There were no airplanes, automobiles, telephones, computers, lightbulbs, televisions, refrigerators, radios, or thousands of other devices used every day. To communicate with their friends, people wrote letters. To travel long distances, they sailed in ships over the ocean. To travel short distances, most people either walked or rode in horse-drawn carriages. All household chores had to be done by hand. Most homes did not have any indoor plumbing or running water, and none had electric outlets or any electrical appliances.

But the world was beginning to change. Shortly before Darwin was born, between 1760 and 1790, England entered into a period of history now known as the Industrial Revolution. This revolution was not a war like the American Revolution or a political upheaval like the French Revolution. It was instead a rapid series of technological and engineering advances that altered how people lived their day-to-day lives.

Steam engines were invented to power machines that could do as much work in an hour as a man could do in a whole day. Iron was used to build bridges and railroads for the first time. Factories sprouted like mushrooms in a landscape that was once entirely covered by farms and forests. Men flocked to the factories to find work, leaving their farms behind. Factory towns grew into cities, and cities grew into huge urban areas. People believed that machines would make England more prosperous and powerful.

In earlier centuries, English society had been sharply divided. At the top were fabulously wealthy aristocrats. At the bottom were the peasants, who were poor, hungry, and downtrodden. There wasn't much aside from these rich and poor social classes. But the Industrial Revolution was changing all that. New classes were arising. Rural peasants became urban factory workers. Middle-class tradesmen made money buying and selling. Highly educated professionals such as doctors, engineers, and lawyers used their skills and expertise to climb high up the social ladder. There were still aristocrats and peasants, of course, but throughout the Industrial Revolution the new middle classes were rapidly growing in size and importance.

These changes also brought problems. Cities became crowded, dirty, and poverty-stricken. The poor were still poor—they just had different jobs, in uglier surroundings. There were not yet any rules or laws about how much workers should be paid or how they should be treated. As a result, workers were often paid as little as possible for working long hours under dangerous conditions. They started to complain, demanding higher wages and more rights. Meanwhile, starving people wanted handouts from the government. The upper classes felt that feeding the poor didn't solve poverty; it only created more poor people in the long run. These social crises frequently threatened to boil over. Riots were common. (It was against this backdrop that Malthus wrote his famous book about overpopulation.)

Children rarely went to school; there were very few schools in all of England! Children with wealthy parents (such as the Darwins) were taught by private tutors and attended expensive boarding schools

and exclusive universities. But most children—starting at 8 or 9 years old—had no choice but to work in coal mines or factories. Without an education they had little chance of ever getting better jobs.

Charles Darwin's family was far away from most of the problems of the era. Both of his grandfathers—Erasmus Darwin and Josiah Wedgwood—were wealthy, as were his father and mother. Throughout Charles's life, he lived in homes full of servants who cooked the meals, tended the gardens, watched the babies, cleaned the rooms, and washed the clothes. But in his autobiography he made almost no mention of this fact. It was as if the servants were invisible. Like most wealthy gentlemen of the 19th century, he assumed that this detail would not need to be explained to his readers. Later in this book, when you read that Charles and Emma Darwin had *10* children, you might wonder how he could manage to raise all those children and be a full-time scientist at the same time. It's simple: the Darwin house (like most upper-class 19th-century houses) was filled with nannies and nurses and governesses to take care of the children. These employees went about their business unnoticed and unmentioned.

Throughout this time, British explorers, armies, and missionaries traveled all over the world. Britain founded colonies and conquered nations on every continent. Wealth and goods from this new British Empire flowed back to England, making it the richest and most powerful country in the world

Revolutionaries tried to overthrow the British social system. Gatherings frequently turned into riots.

Facts, Theories, and Beliefs

Darwin and his theory have always been controversial. But part of the controversy comes from people not understanding the difference between facts, theories, and beliefs.

A **fact** is a piece of information that can be tested or documented, such as a scientific observation or a historical event.

A **theory** is a general principle created to explain a group of tested and documented facts and observations.

A **belief** is a statement of faith that an idea is true or important, whether or not there is any testable evidence for it.

Confusion arises because the word *theory* usually refers to science, while the word *belief* often refers to religion. A scientist is convinced that a theory is correct because it is the best way to explain known facts. A religious person holds a belief because he or she *feels* that it is true, or because a holy person or document says it is true. A religious belief can never be proved—or disproved. Only a fact can be proved. Even a theory can only be *confirmed,* not proved.

The real difference between religious beliefs and scientific theories is that beliefs cannot be questioned or challenged because they are seen as coming from God. Theories, on the other hand, are continuously adjusted and updated to take into account newly discovered facts. And if a new fact completely contradicts an existing theory, then the theory is discarded in favor of a new theory that better explains all the facts.

Since religious beliefs are not based on the world of science at all, people can believe in scientific theories and be religious at the same time. There is nothing about one side that automatically excludes the other. Many scientists believe in God, and most religious people accept some aspects of science. But a scientist could never prove that a religious belief is "wrong," or that God does not exist. In a similar way, a religious person cannot prove that a scientific theory such as evolution is false simply by announcing that God or a holy text doesn't agree with it.

Victoria was only 18 years old when she became Queen of England in 1837.

during the 1800s. As poor as most Britons were, people in other countries were even poorer.

In 1837 a new queen was crowned—Victoria. She was such a beloved leader, and she ruled for such a long time (64 years, until 1901), that the time of her reign is called the Victorian Era. In England during this period, etiquette and proper manners dominated people's relationships. Everything was supposed to be done in a certain way; free-thinking people were not trusted. The fashions and speech of Victorian England are reflected in the stories of Charles Dickens and the Sherlock Holmes mysteries, which were both written in those times.

Throughout Darwin's lifetime, many aspects of English society were seen as getting stronger, bigger, and better than ever before. Despite all the difficulties it brought for workers, the Industrial Revolution was seen as progress, and to the Victorian mind progress was always good. The common attitude at that time was that mankind ruled over the beasts, the rich ruled over the poor, and the Europeans ruled over the rest of the world. Christianity was still seen as the one true religion, and any challenge to the Bible was seen as a challenge to the structure of society.

How ironic it was that someone who benefited greatly from the system—a wealthy and contented gentleman who had studied to be a minister—would be the one to pose its greatest challenge.

2

A Comfortable Youth

Famous Grandfathers: Erasmus Darwin and Josiah Wedgwood

Even before Charles Darwin was born, the name Darwin was one of the most famous in England. Erasmus Darwin, Charles's grandfather, was considered a genius and was one of the first people ever to formulate a theory of ... evolution! It was different from the theory accepted today, but it goes to show that the Darwins had been thinking about evolution for a long time.

Erasmus Darwin (1731–1802) was a skilled doctor who became very popular when he cured a boy thought to have been near death. People believed his treatment was miraculous, but Erasmus merely realized that earlier doctors had misdiagnosed the boy's illness. Even so, patients flocked to his practice in the town of Lichfield, in central England. He started to do so well financially that he not only refused to take money from poorer patients, but instead gave *them* money and food after he cured them! His reputation as the most generous man in the county of Staffordshire grew, along with his fame as a talented physician. One day the King of England, George III, asked Erasmus to become his personal doctor. To everyone's surprise, Erasmus said no because he didn't want to move to London to be near the king. But the fact that Erasmus secretly supported the American colonists in their upcoming revolution against King George may have also influenced his decision.

Erasmus was so fat that he had a semicircle cut out of his dinner table to make room for his stomach and allow him to get closer to the food. Yet his size did not stop him from having many girlfriends

Erasmus Darwin, Charles's grandfather.

while he was in college and later. He married a young lady named Mary Howard, with whom he soon had five children (including one called Robert who in turn became Charles's father). After Mary Howard died while still young, Erasmus had two more children with another girlfriend, and then a few years later he married a second wife who bore him seven more children—a total of 14 in all!

Around 1760 Erasmus met a new patient named Josiah Wedgwood, a young businessman from a family that made pottery—cups, dishes, and kitchenware. The two men quickly became best friends as they shared an interest in steam engines and other mechanical devices that were then being invented in that part of England. This was the start of the Industrial Revolution, when hundreds of new mechanical devices changed society. To Erasmus and Josiah, every new invention was fascinating. And they were right in the middle of all the action. Erasmus himself became an inventor, designing a new kind of windmill for Josiah's pottery factory, as well as a way to steer horse-drawn carriages so they wouldn't tip over (a common problem in those days). But some of his most amazing inventions were never built, because he kept them secret, fearing that someone would steal his ideas. Incredibly, Erasmus even designed steam-powered automobiles and airplanes—decades before anyone else dared to try the idea! The principle behind his steering invention, in fact, is still used today in all modern cars.

Together, Erasmus and Josiah joined a club of scientists, inventors, and thinkers. They named it the Lunar Society because they met once a month during the full moon; the extra light made it easier to get home after the late-night meetings. As a joke, the members started referring to themselves as Lunatics. (In the old days, people used to believe that the full moon made people act insane.) During the 1770s some of the smartest men in England were members, including James Watt, who perfected the steam engine, and Joseph Priestly, the famed chemist who discovered oxygen and many other gases. (He also invented the eraser!) Even Benjamin Franklin visited the club when he came to England as a representative of the American colonists.

The members of the Lunar Society all opposed slavery, supported American independence, and

The Wedgwood family. Josiah Wedgwood, Charles Darwin's grandfather, is sitting at the far right. Susannah Wedgwood, who would become Charles's mother, is the woman sitting on the horse in the center.

believed in religious freedom. These ideas were considered very extreme at the time, so many of the Lunatics kept their political beliefs secret. But mostly they talked about science and the emerging revolution in machinery.

Meeting with all these brilliant minds every month filled Erasmus and Josiah with energy and ideas. Josiah made so many clever improvements to his pottery factory that he became the most successful potter in the country. Even nowadays people still consider Wedgwood pottery as the best ever made. Erasmus started writing books about science and nature. Actually, they weren't regular books but very long poems about animals and medicine and inventions and the future. He had always been better at writing verse than he had been at writing prose, so he found it easier to write down his ideas as poetry rather than in ordinary sentences.

This way of writing may seem strange to modern readers, but in the 18th century people loved it. Erasmus quickly became one of the most famous poets of his day. Yet his skill as a poet overshadowed the topics of his poetry. People were so busy praising *how* he expressed his ideas that few paid attention to *what* his ideas were. He discussed his thoughts about evolution in two poems, one called *Zoönomia* and another called *The Temple of Nature,* in which he wrote:

> Organic life beneath the shoreless waves
> Was born and nurs'd in ocean's pearly caves;
> First forms minute, unseen by spheric glass,
> Move on the mud, or pierce the watery mass;
> These, as successive generations bloom,

New powers acquire and larger limbs assume;
Whence countless groups of vegetation spring,
And breathing realms of fin and feet and wing.

This poem says that life first appeared as microscopic organisms in the ocean and that all the plants and animals that exist today evolved from those first specks of "organic life." Most scientists now believe that all of this is indeed true, but few people realize that it was Erasmus Darwin who first proposed it. History has been unfair to poor Erasmus; he rarely gets credit for his ideas.

But we do know one thing. His grandson, Charles, was inspired by both *Zoönomia* and *The Temple of Nature.* And he ensured that no one would ever forget the name Darwin.

Baby Charles

Erasmus Darwin's son Robert met and fell in love with Josiah Wedgwood's daughter Susannah. In fact, the famous fathers had been secretly hoping for years that their children would become a couple! Robert Darwin also became a doctor, like his father, and grew just as fat. But he was never much interested in poetry or engineering.

After his marriage in 1796, Robert built a large house called The Mount near Shrewsbury in northwestern England and settled in for a comfortable life as a successful country physician. Charles later said that he greatly loved his father, but most people found "Dr. Robert" (as he was called) hard to get along with and a bit scary. Dr. Robert was so large and so opinionated and so strict that people usually fell silent when he came into the room. This was also partly because he was very good at knowing what people were thinking. He could always tell when someone was lying or exaggerating—a skill that made everyone uncomfortable. But his patients found Dr. Robert's skills very helpful, and they often came to tell him about their emotional problems instead of their physical problems. He ended up working half the time as a sort of unofficial psychiatrist. This was fine with Dr. Robert, since—despite being a doctor—he couldn't stand the sight of blood!

Dr. Robert and Susannah had four daughters (Marianne, Caroline, Susan, and Catherine) and two sons. One was named Erasmus after his grandfather, and in 1809 Charles was born. He was to become the most famous Darwin of all.

As a little boy, Charles loved to collect things like shells, rocks, stamps, and coins. Later in life he often wondered if he had traveled the world collecting shells and rocks (and fossils and animals) just so he could continue the games he used to play as a child.

The young Charles also frequently told strange fibs, just so he could stir up excitement. He once sneaked outside, stole an armload of fruit from his

Dr. Robert Darwin, Charles's father.

The Mount, the house where Charles Darwin was born in Shrewsbury.

Be a Backyard Naturalist

One of Charles Darwin's favorite hobbies as a youngster was observing the animals in the countryside around his home. You too can become a backyard naturalist.

What you need
a pencil or pen for writing, and possibly
   colored pens or pencils for drawing
a writing pad, or sheets of blank paper
scissors
glue
stapler

The one thing that any naturalist really needs is *patience*. In order to observe nature, naturalists often have to sit still and be perfectly quiet for long periods of time so as not to disturb the animals they're watching.

Choose a place near your home that has grass, trees, plants, bugs, and animals. The easiest place is your backyard if you have one, or your front yard, or a friend's backyard, or a neighborhood park.

Warm, sunny days are best, because animals like to come out in the sun, and because you wouldn't want to sit outside in the cold.

Find a comfortable location with a good view of places where animals might be. Sit very still for ten minutes and try to observe every animal and insect that you can see. Look for birds, cats, squirrels, spiders, worms, bees, flies, beetles, and anything else that flies, crawls, or walks by. Write down on your pad each type of animal that you see. Instead of just writing "bird," write "Robin, silver-gray wings, orange chest, pale yellow under tail. About 10-inch wingspan. Seems to have injured foot." Try to write down as much detail as you can. If you see two blue jays or two squirrels fighting with each other, describe the fight. Look high in the sky for hawks. Peer into the grass to see ants or centipedes. If any animal stays still long enough, try drawing a sketch of it. Try your best to be accurate.

Once you've made several hours' worth of observations over a few days, take all your "field notes" and make a page about each type of animal, summarizing all your observations. Use one blank sheet for each animal. Cut out and glue your drawings onto each animal's page. Then organize the sheets into groupings—"Birds," "Insects," etc.—and staple them together along the left edge to make your own book.

Charles Darwin at the age of 7, in 1816. He was already interested in nature—notice that he's holding a plant! The girl on the right side of the picture is his sister Catherine.

father's orchard, hid it in a bush, and then ran inside yelling that he had found a secret stash of fruit stolen by a thief! Dr. Robert, of course, saw right through the story, and he was not amused. Another time, Charles claimed that if he watered flowers with colored liquid, the blossoms would come up different colors.

Charles did not go to kindergarten or a regular elementary school; such things did not exist in England at that time. Instead, when he was about

seven years old, Charles began taking lessons from his older sister Caroline, who was a teenager. But, like most teenagers, she had little patience for a restless young boy and often scolded him.

Historians know very little about Charles's mother, Susannah, because she died of stomach problems when Charles was only eight years old, and he grew up remembering almost nothing about her. The young children were not allowed to see her when she was sick, and after she died Dr. Robert would not let anyone in the family ever speak of her again. And even though everyone in the house was very sad, they had to obey their stern father.

Psychologists now think that people should always talk about their feelings, especially when they feel bad. Children who are not allowed to express their emotions about a tragedy sometimes feel awful about it the rest of their lives. Many people feel this is what happened to poor Charles. He must have felt terrible about his mother dying, but he was forced to keep all of his feelings bottled up inside. Is it surprising that he spent most of his life thinking that he had stomach problems?

A Schoolboy

After his mother died, Charles was enrolled in a nearby school for young children, but he hardly learned anything there. The "school" was more like what we would now call a day-care center. He only attended for a year. In 1818, when Charles was

Acquired Characteristics

As you learned in Chapter 1, many 19th-century scientists believed that "acquired characteristics"—features that organisms acquire during their lives—were passed on to offspring. Even Darwin, as a child, claimed he could make flowers turn colors by watering them with colored water. In this experiment you can answer the questions yourself: Can acquired characteristics be passed on? Do plants inherit features acquired by the seeds from which they sprouted?

What you need

spoons

plate (glass or metal)

bottles of food coloring (three or more colors)

a packet of radish seeds

several small plant pots, or empty yogurt
    containers with holes poked in the bottoms

several plastic plant labels or popsicle sticks

soil

Any kind of seeds will do, but radish seeds are the best because they sprout quickly. Look for food coloring in your kitchen, or buy a package with four different colors.

Put a spoon flat on the plate, and squeeze a couple drops of one color of food coloring into it; then take two radish seeds and drop them into the spoon. Repeat the process with all the different colors you have, each in a different spoon with two new seeds. If you only have two or three colors, you can combine one drop of each to make a new color: add blue to red to make purple, and so on. Allow the radish seeds to soak up the color.

Take your small plant pots (or yogurt containers) and fill them most of the way with loose soil, and pat it down. If you have two seeds being dyed red, for example, take two plant labels or popsicle sticks and write "Red" on each one and stick them into the dirt, one for each pot. Repeat the process for each color until you have a row of pots all identified according to color.

Then, one by one, pick up each dyed seed and place it into an appropriately labeled pot. Push each seed about a quarter inch below the soil level and smooth it over. Place the pots in a sunny location, preferably on a tray or dish. Water the seeds thoroughly at first, and every day sprinkle a little water to keep the soil moist (but not soggy).

Now for the hardest part: wait! Radish seeds usually sprout in less than a week—sometimes in as little as two or three days. When the seeds sprout, will their leaves match the colors on the labels? Did the food coloring soak into the seeds and permanently dye the plants? Or will all the sprouts be green, as usual?

Once you've completed this activity, you'll know whether or not environmental influences directly alter basic genetic structure.

nine years old, Dr. Robert decided it was time to finally send him to a real school. Because there were no free public schools in Shrewsbury, Dr. Robert enrolled Charles in an expensive private boys' academy called the Shrewsbury Grammar School. (Charles was lucky to come from a well-off family; in 1818, most boys never had a chance to go to school at all!)

Shrewsbury Grammar School, despite being a long way from London, was actually one of the most well-respected schools in the country. A new headmaster (principal) named Reverend Samuel Butler

Shrewsbury Grammar School.

Making Shrewsbury Cakes

The English food of Darwin's era was very heavy by current standards. Most main dishes involved huge amounts of meat, and recipes often contained fat, "sweetbreads" (a euphemism for animal glands and brains), congealed blood, calves' feet, and other ingredients that people today rarely eat. Very few spices and vegetables were available, and eating dishes from other countries—such as Chinese food or Mexican food—was unheard-of in England. Heavy British cuisine was the only choice.

But not *all* food back then was awful. Darwin particularly liked sweet pastries, and his hometown of Shrewsbury was famous for its delicious cakes and cookies. Here's an authentic recipe from 1808 for one of young Darwin's favorite snacks.

Shrewsbury Cakes
What you need
½ cup (120 ml) butter
¾ cup (180 ml) sugar
1 egg
1 teaspoon (5 ml) rosewater (or vanilla extract, or lemon extract)
1¾ (420 ml) cup flour
½ teaspoon (2.5 ml) nutmeg
¼ teaspoon (1 ml) mace or cinnamon

(Note: Food measurements in those days were very approximate. Feel free to use a little more or less flour or spices until you feel the mixture is just right.)

Take the butter out of the refrigerator and let it warm up to room temperature. Turn on the oven to 350°F (175°C). Put the sugar and the butter into a bowl and whip them together with a fork or beater until they make a light, creamy mixture. Stir in the egg and the rosewater until well blended. (The authentic recipe uses rosewater, but this is hard to find nowadays; you can use vanilla or lemon extract instead.) Sift the flour into a separate bowl with the nutmeg and mace (or cinnamon). Carefully pour the dry ingredients into the wet ingredients and stir until smooth. Place the bowl of dough into the refrigerator. While the dough is cooling, sprinkle some flour on a cutting board and grease a cookie pan with a little butter. Take out the dough, place it on the cutting board, and roll it into a flat sheet about ½ inch (1.3 cm) thick, using a rolling pin, or a tall, straight glass, or a bottle sprinkled with flour. Cut circles out of the flat dough, using either the top of a glass or a cookie cutter. Take the leftover dough, roll it out again, and make more circles until it's all gone. Place the circles on the cookie pan, and bake in the preheated oven for about 10 minutes. Take the "cakes" (they're actually more like cookies) out while they are still light-colored, before they start to turn brown.

Roll out the dough, then use a glass to cut out cookies.

had turned the school into a very strict, no-nonsense preparatory academy. By the time Charles arrived, the Shrewsbury Grammar School, which most people called simply "Dr. Butler's," was a fearsome place. Boys were beaten for not doing their homework or for getting bad grades on tests!

Luckily for Charles, his older brother Erasmus had already been a student there for four years. Erasmus took Charles under his wing and showed him the ropes. But Charles was still a little boy at heart. Even though Dr. Butler's was a boarding school that required all the students to sleep there, little Charles ran home at least once a day, since the Mount was only a mile from the school. He'd stay at home and play with his sisters as long as possible, and then run back to the school as fast as he could at the last minute, dashing inside just before the doors were locked at night. He and Erasmus (whom everybody called by his nickname "Ras," to distinguish him from his grandfather and other relatives who had also been named Erasmus) had to share a bed in a stuffy room with 30 other boys. Since the school didn't have indoor plumbing or bathrooms, all the boys had to use chamber

Charles loved to explore the riverbank behind his house. The Mount can be seen here overlooking the River Severn.

pots as toilets. These were stored under their beds even when they were full. Every morning, the room smelled so bad that even many years later Charles still got sick to his stomach just thinking about it.

Not Much of a Student

You might think that Charles Darwin, who would later be praised as one of the great geniuses of history, was an outstanding student. Yet the opposite is true. By his own admission, Charles was an awful student. He didn't pay attention in class, he copied from his fellow students whenever possible, and he forgot everything he had learned after a day or two. In his autobiography, Charles wrote:

> Nothing could have been worse for the development of my mind than Dr. Butler's school, as it was strictly classical, nothing else being taught except a little ancient geography and history. The school as a means of education to me was simply a blank.

By the phrase "strictly classical," Charles meant that the only topics taught at the school were the ancient languages of Latin and Greek. No English, no science, no sports, no recent history, no other languages; it was Latin and Greek and nothing else. You can imagine why Charles hated it, especially since he was terrible at learning foreign languages.

During days off Charles could always be found outside, collecting birds' eggs, newts, and bugs; fish-ing; playing with dogs; and running through the fields. Nowadays people think of Darwin as a serious old man who locked himself in his room and wrote books without ever budging from his chair, but when he was young he was very active and free-spirited, and could hardly stand to be cooped up indoors for any period of time.

When Charles was around 14, his father allowed him to get a rifle. Dr. Robert wanted the family to be seen as part of a wealthy social set, and hunting was the main hobby of upper-class gentlemen who lived in the countryside. So he allowed Darwin to go hunting with his uncles and other family members at first, and later by himself. But Dr. Robert soon came to regret his decision, because Charles loved shooting so much more than he liked his studies. For a while, Charles talked about nothing else but hunting birds in the woods around Shrewsbury. One day, angry at Charles's nonstop hunting and terrible performance at school, Dr. Robert yelled at him, "You care for nothing but shooting, dogs, and rat-catching, and you will be a disgrace to yourself and all your family." Charles felt so bad about the scolding that he never forgot it for the rest of his life.

But even when Charles became interested in serious subjects, he was still criticized. Sometime around 1824, Ras convinced Dr. Robert to let him and Charles build a homemade chemistry lab in a toolshed at the Mount. There the boys put together a very impressive collection of equipment (it helped to be from a wealthy family). They started telling the other boys at school about their chemistry experiments, and Charles earned a new nickname:

"Gas." When Dr. Butler found out what was going on, he scolded Charles in front of the whole school for wasting his time on "useless subjects."

By 1825, Dr. Robert and Dr. Butler sadly realized that Charles was "a very ordinary boy, rather below the common standard in intellect." In other words, Charles was too dumb for Shrewsbury Grammar School. So his father, to avoid further embarrassment, took Charles out of school at the age of 16.

Off to College

What to do with a good-for-nothing boy like Charles Darwin? His father was in a foul mood about Charles's poor performance in school.

Ras was 20 by that time, and he had already studied medicine for a few years at Cambridge University. But he was transferring that month to the famous medical school at Edinburgh in Scotland, where he would start his final training to become a doctor, just as his father and grandfather had done. Dr. Robert decided the best thing to do was send Charles to join Ras at Edinburgh University, where they would *both* study medicine.

Edinburgh University was the leading medical college in the country at the time, so how could Charles, who performed poorly in school, gain admission to the best college? Things were much different in those days. In the modern world, there is a great deal of competition to get into good colleges. Only the best students are allowed into the top schools. Today, a bad student such as Charles would have to settle for a very unimportant college, or no college at all. But in 1825, there were no academic requirements to enter most of the top universities. It didn't matter what your previous grades were, or if you had even gone to school. All that mattered was whether you could afford to pay the tuition fees. Most families couldn't possibly afford all the expenses at Edinburgh University. But Dr. Robert made good money as a doctor and made clever investments as well, so he could easily send both his sons to college. (Charles's four sisters could *not* attend; girls weren't allowed to go to college in those days.) So, even though Charles was not really old enough or well educated enough to go to college, in October 1825, at the age of 16, he packed his bags and set off for Edinburgh.

Once there, he and Ras rented rooms together near the university. Charles in particular was excited by the hustle and bustle of the big city. Edinburgh was very sophisticated compared to Shrewsbury, and the air was filled with new ideas. He wrote breathless letters home during his first few months there. He signed up for as many classes as he could and he checked out piles of books from the school library.

As his first school year dragged on, however, Charles found the lectures to be terribly boring—except for chemistry, which he still liked because of the experiments he and Ras had done at home. Maybe he was bored with his other classes because he was too young to understand the lessons, or maybe the professors were dull; it was probably a little of both.

Erasmus Darwin, Charles's brother.

The last straw came when Charles, like all young medical students, was required to watch an actual surgery in progress. Horrible as it may be to imagine, in the early 1800s there were no anesthetics, the medicines used to keep patients from feeling pain. Patients in those days were conscious as doctors operated on them, and could feel the knife cutting into their skin. Furthermore, surgeons didn't even wash their hands beforehand, so after an agonizing operation—even if it was successful—patients often died of infections.

The day Charles came to watch an operation, the patient was a young child. The child screamed so loudly and thrashed around so desperately that assistants had to hold the child down as the doctor started cutting. Blood was spurting everywhere. Charles was completely horrified and had to run out the room to avoid getting sick or fainting. He knew from that day forward that he could never be a doctor.

After this experience, Charles was in a dilemma. Ras had convinced Charles that someday both of them would inherit plenty of money from their wealthy father. They agreed that there was no point in becoming doctors if they were going to be rich anyway. That was a lazy and greedy thought, Charles later admitted, yet it was quite tempting for a spoiled 17-year-old. But if Dr. Robert found out that Charles had dropped out of medical school, he'd be so furious that he might cut Charles out of his will. So Charles decided to be both lazy *and* sneaky; he would stay in school but not really pay attention to his classes anymore. He simply couldn't tell his father that he was no longer interested in

becoming a doctor. He would just *pretend* to be a medical student. In truth, he had lost all interest in school.

Ras graduated that year and halfheartedly took on a few patients, but his career as a doctor didn't last long. He followed his own advice: he quit being a doctor, moved to London, and spent the rest of his life living off the money he got from his father.

By modern standards, Ras turned out to be a bit of a do-nothing. Yet his lifestyle was in fact very common in those days. If one was wealthy enough to live comfortably, there seemed no point in working. And there was no shame in this at all. A man who didn't need to have a job was considered a respectable gentleman. And Charles seemed destined to follow in Ras's footsteps. He just didn't want his father to find out.

So that first summer vacation after Edinburgh, Charles hardly went home at all, and spent months visiting relatives, hunting, and taking hiking trips in Wales. He still was intensely interested in natural history, and he continued collecting all sorts of birds and bugs. That summer he read a book called *The Natural History of Birds,* and it made him a little ashamed that he hunted birds for sport instead of for scientific reasons. That summer he also read his grandfather Erasmus's poem *Zoönomia,* which may for the first time have set Charles to thinking about evolution.

The second year at Edinburgh, Charles ignored his medical classes and instead focused almost entirely on his new interest, science. He joined a student club called the Plinian Society that discussed the latest scientific breakthroughs. He made many new friends, including a teacher named Robert Grant. Everyone else thought Grant was unfriendly, but Charles liked him. Grant had a very active imagination underneath his grumpy personality. Together they took many walks along the seashore, searching for interesting animal specimens. Darwin would try to cut open these specimens and see what was inside, but because he had skipped all his anatomy classes, he wasn't very good at dissecting things.

On one of their walks, Grant suddenly turned to Charles and started talking excitedly about evolution. He described in detail the theories of Lamarck, which Charles noticed were exactly like those of his grandfather. In his autobiography Charles later claimed that this incident "made no impression on my mind," but the fact that he remembered it after 50 years meant it probably made a big impression on him. In fact, most historians now think that this was the moment when Charles Darwin started on his course to solve the problem of evolution.

Charles also went out with the local fishermen on their boats to inspect the unusual things they dredged up in their nets. He made some minor discoveries that he described to the Plinian Society. He started to become interested in geology (the study of the Earth) as well, and even tried taking a class in it, but—as usual—he found the class so boring he stopped going.

Instead, Charles attended all sorts of events outside of school. He went to see the famous naturalist and artist John James Audubon give a demonstration on how to stuff dead birds in lifelike poses, a skill called taxidermy. Charles was so fascinated

with it that afterwards he started taking private taxidermy lessons from a man named John Edmonstone, who lived practically next door in Edinburgh. Charles would listen for hours as Edmonstone described his experiences traveling through the jungles of South America with a famous explorer. The two became very close. What makes this remarkable is that John Edmonstone was a former slave and was practically the only black man in all of Scotland! Nothing better demonstrates how liberal and fair-minded Charles Darwin was; most people in Britain in those days wouldn't even dream of becoming friends with a black person.

Charles learned to stuff birds so they looked completely lifelike.

Time for a Change

As his second year at college ended, Charles hadn't made much progress toward getting his degree. He decided to quit school. He still hoped to hide this from his father, but his sisters tattled on him. Charles was in big trouble. "He was very properly vehement against my turning an idle sporting man, which then seemed my probable destination," Charles later wrote.

Desperate to avoid a confrontation with his father, Charles did everything he could to avoid going home. After leaving Edinburgh in April 1827, he traveled around Scotland and Ireland for a while. Then he visited London, and from there took a trip to Paris to visit his cousins from the Wedgwood side of the family, who were on vacation there. Charles had practically grown up with his cousin

Emma Wedgwood, as the Darwins and Wedgwoods frequently stayed at each other's estates for long visits. But it was there in Paris, when they were both 18, that Charles really noticed her for the first time. He wrote a letter to his sisters saying he was amazed at how beautiful Emma had become, now that she was grown up. But they did not fall in love—not yet, at least. Charles realized it was time to finally go home to The Mount and face his father.

But back at home, Charles got the bad news. Dr. Robert had decided that since Charles refused to study medicine, he would have to become a clergyman, a priest in the Church of England. Although it now seems like a very odd job for a nonreligious person such as Charles, there was no arguing with Dr. Robert. So Charles meekly agreed. He was to study at Christ's College in Cambridge for three years, then take a respectable position as a country parson. It wouldn't be so bad, Charles reasoned. Country parsons in those days had very few responsibilities and often spent their time pursuing other hobbies.

Unlike Edinburgh, however, Cambridge *did* have requirements: students wishing to enter religious studies had to be fluent in Latin and Greek! Charles practically cried when he found out. Of all the subjects he hated—and he hated most of them—Latin and Greek were the worst. He had forgotten every word he had ever learned (or had pretended to learn) in grammar school. He would have to start from the beginning. Dr. Robert hired a private tutor, and Charles spent several months learning the classics all over again.

The boredom of studying was broken by a new interest: girls. Forgetting all about his cousin Emma, Charles became infatuated with a pretty and sophisticated girl named Fanny Owen, who was his sisters' friend. Every young man around Shrewsbury had his eye on Fanny, but Charles was persistent. He frequently paid visits to the house where she lived with her father and would take her out to the woods for hunting practice. Most historians now think of Fanny as Charles's first girlfriend.

Finally, after eight long months of agonizing Latin and Greek lessons, Charles was ready to go to Cambridge. He showed up in January of 1828 and started classes.

A Cambridge Varmint

From his very first day at Cambridge, Charles was never serious about studying or becoming a clergyman. He found that there were two kinds of students at Cambridge: "reading men" who were very serious, attended every lecture, and got good grades; and "varmints," unambitious fellows from well-off families who spent their time going to parties and goofing off. Unfortunately, Darwin fell in with the varmints and spent many an evening playing cards and getting drunk. He later wrote, "During the three years which I spent at Cambridge my time was wasted, as far as the academical studies were concerned, as completely as at Edinburgh and at [grammar] school." In truth he wasn't quite as lazy as his friends were; he managed to do just enough work to pass through his term with average grades.

But as his interest in schoolwork dwindled away, his interest in natural history started to grow.

In the 1820s a craze was sweeping England: beetle collecting. It seemed that everyone was suddenly an amateur entomologist (an expert on insects). People competed with each other to gather the biggest and best collection of dead beetles, butterflies, and other bugs. Collectors would even pay high prices for rare species.

At Cambridge, Charles became close friends with another cousin of his who was a fellow student, William Darwin Fox. Fox was deeply involved in the beetle craze, and he invited Charles to join him. As you've seen before (and as you'll see again later in his life), Charles tended to focus intensely on certain things and seemingly ignore everything else, just as he had done with hunting. At Cambridge it happened again. Within weeks he had forgotten about nearly everything but beetles. He was determined to gather the biggest and best collection of rare beetles in the country.

He and Fox would go out "beetling" almost every day, searching for bugs in old tree trunks, under rocks, and everywhere. Charles had become obsessed. One day, searching under a piece of bark, he discovered two very rare beetles. He grabbed one in each hand, but before he could put them in his collecting jar, he saw an even rarer one. Determined not to let the third beetle get away, he popped one of the first two into his mouth, so that he would have a hand free. The bug in his mouth turned out to be a dangerous bombardier beetle, which sprayed a burning, poisonous fluid onto his tongue! He spat out the beetle, lost it, and lost the one he was grabbing for as well.

As usual, Charles avoided all his required classes and instead attended optional classes on topics he found more interesting. His favorite was a class on botany (the study of plants) with a popular teacher named John Stevens Henslow. Darwin would accompany Henslow on field trips to study the plants and animals around Cambridge. Though Henslow was much older, the two became great friends, and more than anybody, Henslow taught Charles how to observe the world with a scientific eye. Charles began to realize that science was not something locked up in a museum but could be found in the world all around him.

Charles Darwin was not yet an old man with a bald head and a long white beard, as most people these days imagine him. During his time at Cambridge he was the age of college students today—he was only 22 when he graduated. Standing more than six feet tall, he had strong muscles and was full of energy. Luckily, he took after his mother's side of the family—the Wedgwoods—when it came to looks, and was fairly handsome with a flat nose, a big forehead, and intelligent eyes. He never grew fat like his father and grandfather. And even though he loved the outdoors, he wore the latest fashions, including big bushy sideburns and a tall top hat.

Throughout the first two years at Cambridge he would go home during vacations and spend time with Fanny. But one Christmas he didn't go home at all, and she was so angry and disappointed that they broke up.

The beetle-collecting craze seized the popular imagination. This cartoon shows a woman of the era whose hair and dress were drawn to look like a beetle.

When he was close to graduating, Charles read a book by an explorer named Alexander von Humboldt describing his travels in the Canary Islands and South America. He was thrilled by Humboldt's adventures. Suddenly Charles was gripped with the frantic desire to go to the Canary Islands and follow in Humboldt's footsteps. When he finally managed to graduate from Cambridge in 1831, the only thing on his mind was voyaging to the tropics. In April he wrote a letter to Fox saying, "I talk, think, and dream of a scheme I have almost hatched of going to the Canary Islands. I have long had a wish of seeing tropical scenery and vegetation." A week later he wrote another letter to his sister Caroline: "In the morning I go and gaze at palm trees in the hot-house and come home and read Humboldt. My enthusiasm is so great that I cannot hardly sit still on my chair." The travel stories of South America that he had heard from the taxidermist John Edmonstone back in Edinburgh also made him hungry for adventure.

Charles started preparing for the trip, even though he had no idea how he was going to get there. He began studying Spanish on his own (since the Canary Islands belonged to Spain). In August he decided to go on another educational field trip with a Cambridge teacher named Adam Sedgwick, who was an expert in geology. Ever since the boring lectures in Edinburgh, Charles had disliked geology, but he wanted to be a top-notch geologist for his trip to the Canary Islands. Sedgwick spent three weeks making careful observations in northern Wales, training Charles how to be a professional scientist. But Charles's favorite time of year—hunting season—started in September, so at the end of August he said goodbye to Sedgwick and went home to Shrewsbury, which was nearby. When he arrived on August 29, 1831, he discovered to his surprise that he had mail waiting for him. As he sat down and opened the envelope, he had no idea that it would change his life—and the history of science—forever.

A Classical Education

Darwin's early schooling focused almost entirely on the classics—the study of ancient Greece and Rome. Like most students at the time, he was also forced to learn the Greek and Latin languages. Although Darwin hated studying these ancient languages, his knowledge of Latin was quite useful later in his research on evolution, because Linnaeus had assigned precise Latin names to every species in the world. Without a detailed knowledge of the Linnean taxonomy system, Darwin could not have developed his theory.

Since many modern words and languages come from Latin, studying it is also a good way to become a linguistic expert! This activity will help you get started.

What you need
a dictionary that includes word derivations

The Romans established a huge empire that covered most of Europe and the Middle East, stretching from Spain to Armenia, and from Scotland to Egypt. And everywhere the Romans went, they brought Latin with them. For over five hundred years it was the main language of the Western world.

Some Latin Vocabulary Words

amicus = friend
aqua = water
bonus = good
domus = house
equus = horse
est = is
et = and
facere = to make
luna = moon
malus = bad
manus = hand
mater = mother
quod = because
sed = but
tempus = time
ubi = where
video = I see

Latin Words You Already Know

Many Latin words and phrases have entered directly into English. Here are some that you've probably heard before:

et cetera (usually abbreviated as "etc.")
et = and, *cetera* = the rest

ad infinitum (meaning "going on forever," or "never ending")
ad = to, *infinitum* = infinity

e pluribus unum (the motto of the United States, printed on all coins)
e = from, *pluribus* = many, *unum* = one (meaning "from many [states] comes one [nation]")

Pronouncing Latin

Latin words are pronounced just as they look on the page. Unlike English, Latin has no silent letters. A few special rules: the letter "c" is always a "hard c" that sounds just like a "k" (as in "can") and never "soft" like an "s" (as in "ice"). The vowels are usually (but not always) "short," so an "a" sounds as it does in "ball," an "e" as in "red," an "i" as in "sit," an "o" as in "hot," and a "u" as in "put."

Some Latin Grammar

Most words in Latin have different endings depending on how they are used in a sentence. People usually find this the most difficult part of learning Latin, because the rules for word endings are very complicated and very strict. Adjectives always have to agree with the nouns they refer to, so a big ball would be *globus magnus,* but a big fire would be *flamma magna.* Notice that *-us* has to go with *-us,* and *-a* has to go with *-a.* Verbs also have different endings and forms, similar to the way "to <u>be</u>" in English becomes "I <u>am</u>," "you <u>are</u>," "he <u>is</u>," and "they <u>were</u>," depending on the subject and the tense.

Some Well-Known Linnean Animal Names in Latin
Darwin knew the Latin taxonomic name for almost every animal and plant. You know some too—maybe without even realizing they are Latin!

Homo sapiens (the official name for human beings):
homo = man, *sapiens* = intelligent, wise

Tyrannosaurus rex (a gigantic carnivorous dinosaur):
tyranno- = tyrant, *saurus* = lizard, *rex* = king

Felis domesticus (a cat—the kind you keep as a pet)
felis = cat, *domesticus* = domestic (i.e., lives in a house)

English Words with Latin Roots
Did you know that over half the words in English are based on Latin? Even common words you would never suspect were Latin, like "nose" (from *nasus,* meaning nose) have ancient origins. Knowing the Latin roots of words not only helps you to understand them better, but also helps you figure out the meanings of words you've never seen before.

"Thermometer," for example, comes from *therm-* meaning heat, and *-meter* meaning measure, so a thermometer is something that measures heat. If you knew Latin, you could have figured out the meaning even if you'd never *heard* of a thermometer! Try looking up these words in your dictionary to see which Latin words they come from (in most dictionaries, the root of the word is usually given in parentheses before the definition):

library
orbit
cry
animal
announce
captain

Before you looked them up, did you know that all these words came from Latin? Most people—even educated adults—would not have known. Don't stop with just these. Spend some time browsing the word derivations in the dictionary—it's like a treasure hunt to find the secret behind every word.

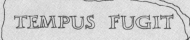

TEMPUS FUGIT

3

To Distant Lands

Darwin's package actually contained two letters: one from Henslow, and the other from another Cambridge professor named George Peacock. Both said the same thing: the British government had asked Peacock to recommend a naturalist to go on an around-the-world trip aboard a ship called the HMS *Beagle*. Not knowing whom to suggest, Peacock had asked Henslow for advice, and Henslow had suggested Charles Darwin, his favorite student. The trip was to take two years, during which time Charles would be expected to collect scientific samples wherever the ship landed. First stop: the Canary Islands!

You can imagine Charles's reaction. It was a dream come true. He ran excitedly to his father, showed him the letters, and said he wanted to go more than anything in the world. Dr. Robert read the letters and scowled. He had just spent five years and a lot of money sending his son to school, train-

ing him to be a doctor and a clergyman. Now Charles wanted to throw it all away and go on a two-year pleasure cruise? *No,* said Dr. Robert. *I forbid you to go. You will get a job with the church as a country parson, settle into your parsonage, and grow up to be a respectable gentleman. No more of these wild schemes of yours.*

Charles was crushed. But he needed his father's permission and support, because the trip was going to cost a lot of money, and Charles still had none of his own. So, that evening, with a heavy heart, Charles sat down and wrote a letter telling Henslow regretfully that he couldn't accept the offer. The letter was mailed immediately.

The next morning Charles felt miserable. His spirit broken, he rode off to go partridge hunting at the Wedgwood house, where his cousins and uncle lived, twenty miles away. Once there, he described to his uncle Josiah Wedgwood (his mother's

At one point while surveying the Argentinian coastline, the *Beagle* had to be dragged ashore so its damaged hull could be repaired. This drawing is based on a description by Captain FitzRoy.

brother) what had happened. "Uncle Jos," as Darwin called him, thought the trip was the chance of a lifetime and was shocked to hear that Dr. Robert had forbidden it. Suddenly, Charles remembered one thing his angry father had said: "If you can find any man of common sense, who advises you to go, I will give my consent." There was no one Dr. Robert respected more than his brother-in-law Josiah. Maybe together, Charles reasoned, they could change Dr. Robert's mind.

Uncle Jos asked Charles to write down all the reasons his father had said "No" to the trip. This is exactly what Charles wrote:

1. *Disreputable to my character as a Clergyman hereafter*
2. *A wild scheme*
3. *That they must have offered to many others before me, the place of Naturalist*
4. *And from its not being accepted there must be some serious objection to the vessel or expedition*
5. *That I should never settle down to a steady life hereafter*
6. *That my accommodation would be most uncomfortable*
7. *That you consider it as again changing my profession*
8. *That it would be a useless undertaking*

Josiah scanned the list and wrote an answer to each point, trying to convince Dr. Robert that he was mistaken. They sent the note back to The Mount. Charles hoped that his father would change his mind.

The next day, he wondered: What if the letter didn't work? They had to go convince his father in person. He and Uncle Jos jumped into a carriage and rushed back to Shrewsbury. When they arrived, Dr. Robert told them he had already written a reply to their letter, stating that he was convinced! Josiah, who definitely had "common sense," was right on every point. Dr. Robert granted Charles permission to go.

Frantic Preparations

Charles was ecstatic. The ship was to leave in a month, and he had so much to do to get ready. Then he remembered that he had already mailed a letter declining the invitation! Frantic, Charles rushed off to Cambridge to tell Henslow he had changed his mind. When he arrived, Henslow told him it was not too late. They had not yet given the job to anyone else. The last step was for Charles to meet with the captain of the *Beagle*, Robert FitzRoy.

Henslow then explained that Charles was asked to go primarily as a companion to the captain. The ship already had an official naturalist—the ship's doctor—but Charles would be allowed to be a naturalist as well, if he wanted. The British navy had very strict rules of etiquette at the time, and they stated that the captain was not allowed to socialize with the crew. Furthermore, Captain FitzRoy was from a very high-class family, and he felt it was improper for him to eat meals with the ship's officers as well, since they were all from middle-

Charles's uncle Josiah Wedgwood, better known as "Uncle Jos."

class or lower-class families. Yet he feared becoming lonely and isolated on a trip that was to last at least two years, and he wanted a companion with whom he could eat, converse, and be friends. So it was extremely important that Charles meet with the captain and get his approval. Henslow also warned Charles that FitzRoy was very conservative politically, that he supported slavery, and that he considered wealthy aristocrats to be naturally superior to everyone else—and that Charles should hide his true feelings and liberal political views.

So Charles met with FitzRoy in London and, despite their differences, they got along well. Even though he had already been a ship's captain for three years, FitzRoy was only 26, just four years older than Charles. And they both were passionately interested in science. Within days, Charles had re-

ceived official word from the government that he could go on the trip.

With no time to lose, Charles rushed around London buying all sorts of scientific equipment for the journey: telescopes, chemicals for preserving specimens, measuring instruments—even pistols, as FitzRoy had said Charles would need them to defend himself from bandits and cannibals! Charles had never been so excited in his life.

The government was sending the *Beagle* to survey the coast of South America, and then continue around the world taking careful measurements of longitude, to make British naval charts more accurate for shipping. The ship had already started this huge task years earlier, but had not completed it. The previous journeys had damaged the ship, and now it was being repaired in Plymouth—the

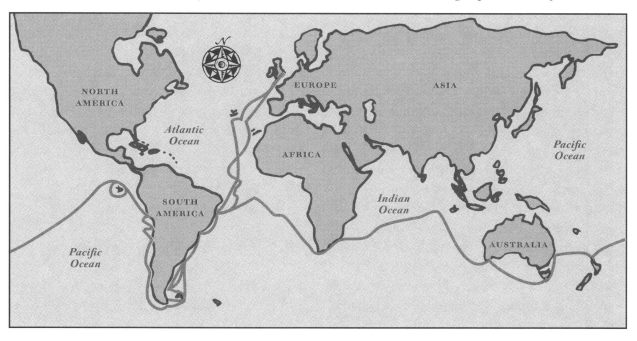

The route of the HMS *Beagle* around the world.

same port from which the Pilgrims had left for North America 200 years earlier.

Darwin accompanied FitzRoy to inspect the ship in mid-September 1831, and got more than his fair share of bad news. First, the ship was nowhere near ready, and the departure date was going to be delayed for at least a month. Second, the time of the journey had been extended to three years, not two. And worst of all, Charles was shocked at how small the ship was. How could the tiny vessel carry 74 men around the world? Like everyone on board the ship, Charles had been given a tiny area in which to sleep. In fact, it wasn't even his private room; he and another man had to sleep in hammocks strung up in the ship's chart room. He was given one small corner in which to stuff all his equipment, and during the day all sorts of people would come in and out of the room on official business. There was absolutely no privacy at all. When he heard the ship's nickname was "the floating coffin," and that it tended to tip over in bad weather, he became even more nervous. It turned out that many of Dr. Robert's objections had been right after all! But there was no backing out now.

The news got even worse. Bad weather repeatedly delayed the ship's departure. Twice it actually set out and was forced to return because the wind was blowing in the wrong direction. It was already near the end of December and the ship was still stuck in port. Charles later wrote, "These two months at Plymouth were the most miserable which I ever spent." It was at this time that Charles first experienced a psychological problem that was to bother him all his life: hypochondria, or the terrible fear

that one is dying of some incurable disease. Referring to this period of anxious waiting, Charles wrote, "I was out of spirits at the thought of leaving all my family and friends for so long a time, and the weather seemed to me inexpressibly gloomy. I was also troubled with palpitations and pain about the heart, and like many a young ignorant man, especially one with a smattering of medical knowledge, was convinced that I had heart disease."

On Christmas Day the entire crew got drunk as a way to blow off steam. The next morning, December 26, the weather was clear for the first time in weeks. Yet the ship couldn't depart because everyone was either asleep or had a terrible hangover! Captain FitzRoy was so angry that he had many of the crewmen publicly beaten and the rest locked up in chains. This greatly upset Charles, and he started to wonder just how well he was going to get along with FitzRoy after all.

Finally, on December 27, 1831, everyone was recovered, the sky was blue, and the ship was ready to sail. The *Beagle* finally sailed out of the harbor that morning, carrying Charles, FitzRoy, and 72 other men on a journey that would eventually last not two years but almost five. (From here on, this book will refer to Charles by his last name only.)

The Voyage Begins

During the earlier attempts to leave port, Darwin had felt a little seasick for the few hours they had been at sea. He knew what he was in for. Shortly

before their final departure, he had written, "I look forward to seasickness with utter dismay." Even so, his stomach was not prepared for life on the open sea. As the *Beagle* headed south it entered rough waters, and the ship pitched and heaved day and night. Charles immediately became so seasick that he threw up almost nonstop for a week. He couldn't eat, sleep, or even stand up. He was beginning to think he had made a terrible mistake.

He finally emerged from his cabin on January 6 as they approached Tenerife, the main Canary Island. Finally! His dream was about to come true. The seasickness almost seemed worth it.

Darwin's joy lasted about half an hour. The Spanish authorities sent a message to the *Beagle* saying that no ships from England would be allowed to land. There was news of a cholera epidemic in Britain, and the Spanish authorities didn't want British sailors bringing the disease to the Canaries. They said the ship would have to wait offshore in quarantine for at least twelve days.

FitzRoy was outraged. He ordered the ship to continue on its journey without ever stopping at the Canary Islands after all. You can imagine Darwin's disappointment as the islands disappeared in the distance. The whole reason he had agreed to the trip in the first place was to visit these very islands, and now his only chance to see them was lost.

The *Beagle* sailed south and a short time later stopped instead at the Cape Verde Islands, which like the Canaries are off the coast of Africa. Darwin finally got to go ashore. It was everything he had hoped for. He later wrote:

Here I first saw the glory of tropical vegetation. Tamarinds, bananas and palms were flourishing at my feet. I returned to the shore, treading on volcanic rocks, hearing the notes of unknown birds, seeing new insects fluttering about still newer flowers. It has been for me a glorious day, like giving sight to a blind man's eyes.

He also noticed, about 45 (14 m) feet above sea level, a white stripe running through the rock all the way around the island. Upon closer inspection, he saw that the white stripe contained fossilized shells, and that the rock layers above and below were hardened lava. This started Darwin to thinking: How did the shells get so far above the sea? Before they departed, Captain FitzRoy had given him a newly published book called *Principles of Geology*, by the famous geologist Charles Lyell. In this book—now considered one of the most important books of the 19th century—Lyell first proposed that the Earth is many millions of years old, and that it has been slowly shaped by geological processes that eventually created the landscape as we see it today. (See Chapter 4 for more information on Lyell.) Darwin had already read *Principles of Geology* by the time he saw the white stratum. The unusual formation hatched ideas in his mind; maybe Lyell was right. Obviously, Darwin reasoned, the shells had originally been on the ocean floor. Then a layer of hot lava poured over them and baked them white. Then, over a long period of time, the same volcano that had ejected the lava caused the sea floor to slowly rise. Eventually it rose above the surface of the sea and became an island. Prior

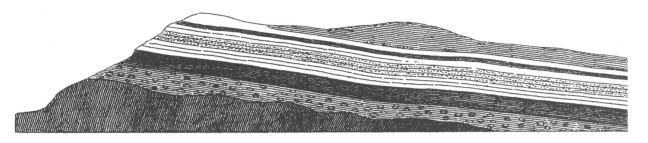

Darwin saw a white stratum similar to the ones depicted here.

to Lyell, most people thought the Earth was unchanging, that it was in the same shape now that it had always been. That concept just didn't make sense, Darwin thought, eyeing the white stripe. Another theory, called *catastrophism,* was that the Earth had indeed changed, but very violently and rapidly, and over only a 6,000-year span, to match the chronology of the Bible. That didn't make sense either, considering the lazy way the stripe wandered up and down; there was nothing to suggest fast or violent change.

Darwin didn't spend much time on the Cape Verde Islands, but they did give him his first taste of the tropics and his first scientific speculations. Next, the *Beagle* headed straight across the Atlantic to Brazil, stopping to hunt for sharks to eat along the way. The sea was smoother now, and although Darwin was still seasick at times, it wasn't nearly as bad as it had been during those first few weeks. When the ship crossed the equator, Darwin and all the others on board who had never before crossed it had to endure a traditional sailors' ritual in which they were blindfolded, covered in tar and paint, and dunked in the water. Captain FitzRoy dressed up in costume as King Neptune

and led the ritual, which soon turned into a childish water fight, soaking everyone.

South America at Last

Finally they arrived at Bahia (now named Salvador), Brazil, on February 28, 1832. Darwin could hardly believe what he saw. The jungles of Brazil, laid out before him, were overwhelming—a naturalist's paradise. After his first day ashore, he wrote,

> The delight one experiences in such times bewilders the mind. If the eye attempts to follow the flight of a gaudy butterfly, it is arrested by some strange tree or fruit; if watching an insect one forgets it in the stranger flower it is crawling over.... Delight itself, however, is a weak term to express the feelings of a naturalist who, for the first time, has been wandering by himself in a Brazilian forest.

The crew of the *Beagle* hunting for sharks near St. Paul's Rocks, small islands in the middle of the Atlantic Ocean.

Botanical Treasure Hunt

When Darwin landed in South America he encountered for the first time all kinds of plants and foods he had never seen or tasted before. Nowadays, all sorts of exotic and unusual fruits and vegetables are easy to find near your home. You don't need to travel around the world to discover new foods!

What you need
a notepad and pencil
an adult to accompany you

Start your botanical treasure hunt in your local supermarket. Go to the section with fresh fruits and vegetables. Skip the apples and onions and search for fruits and vegetables you've never eaten before. Does the store have guavas, plantains, arugula, or parsnips? Write down the name of each new fruit or vegetable, and underneath carefully describe each one. What color is it? What shape? How does it smell? Is it squishy or firm? Ask the grocer where some of them are grown. If you have the time, try drawing a sketch of each kind.

But not all supermarkets have unusual foods. Ask an adult to take you to markets that sell products from different countries, or from cultures different from your family's. America has many ethnic communities from all over the world. Depending on where you live, you might find markets that sell foods from Mexico, China, Russia, Jamaica, Colombia, Vietnam, the Middle East, Guatemala, India, Ethiopia, Thailand, and many other places. Go adventuring! See how many amazing and un-

usual fruits and vegetables you can find in each store, and take notes on every kind. And ask your parents to buy some of the ones that interest you the most, so you can see what they taste like.

Research each kind of plant to learn where it comes from and how it is eaten. Then, using all the information you've collected, write a separate page for each fruit and vegetable, including your sketches if possible. Arrange the pages in alphabetical order and staple them together to make a book of your discoveries.

He immediately reverted to his favorite hobby—collecting beetles. He also captured and brought back to the ship other insects, birds, and lizards. What pleased Darwin most of all was that it was now his *job* to be a collector. His father had always treated Darwin's interest in nature as a waste of time, something Darwin did to fill the days before settling down in a real profession. But here in South America, being a naturalist *was* his profession. He no longer had to feel guilty about it. There in the jungles of Brazil, he realized how he wanted to spend his life.

Darwin was lucky to have landed in Brazil during Carnival. As far back as the 1830s and earlier, this was the country's biggest celebration, with parades and parties every night. Even so, Darwin didn't feel much like celebrating. He saw something else he'd never seen before, and it made him very angry: slavery. Black slaves brought over from Africa worked on the docks in Bahia, where they were treated badly and not paid for their labor. Seeing the slaves suffer put Darwin in a foul mood.

Back on the ship, Darwin told Captain FitzRoy how much he hated slavery, saying that he wished all slaves could be set free. FitzRoy had a different opinion. He told Darwin that black people lived better lives as slaves in South America than they did back home in Africa. In fact, FitzRoy said, he had once visited a plantation where the owner called in all of his slaves and asked them if they'd like to go free. They all answered "No"—they said they were happier as slaves. FitzRoy felt he had proven his point, but Darwin replied, What would you expect slaves to say in front of their master? If they had said they wanted to go free, they would have been whipped or put in shackles.

The *Beagle*'s crewmen had previously warned Darwin about FitzRoy's temper. The captain even had a nickname, "Hot Coffee," since he always boiled over. Yet it was not until this minute that Darwin experienced one of his moods full force. FitzRoy flew into a rage. No one was ever allowed to argue with the captain! He banished Darwin from his dining area and ordered Darwin never to speak to him again. Furthermore, he said, perhaps it was time for Darwin to pack up and go home.

For a few hours, Darwin thought his adventure was over. Luckily, FitzRoy soon calmed down, took back everything he had said and told Darwin to forget about the fight. But Darwin had learned a lesson: never, *ever* talk about slavery or politics to FitzRoy. From that day onward, he watched his words very carefully. Even years later, after Darwin was a world-famous scientist, he made sure never to say anything in public that might cause an argument.

After a short stay in Bahia, the *Beagle* continued onward down the coast of Brazil to the large city of Rio de Janiero.

In Rio, the first shipment of mail (sent on a fast ship from England) was awaiting the *Beagle*. Darwin's sisters wrote that his ex-girlfriend, Fanny, was getting married to someone else! The news made him very sad. His dreams of maybe getting back together with her were gone. From that day forward, he would live for science.

When they arrived in Rio, Darwin was invited by a local landowner to visit his ranch deep in the

The jungles of Brazil, as Darwin saw them.

Darwin visited a Brazilian plantation like this one.

interior of Brazil. Darwin agreed, but sorely regretted it after seven days of riding nonstop through the wilderness. Once they arrived, Darwin discovered that the ranch was actually a plantation with many slaves working there. The landowner soon got into an argument with the man he had hired to run the plantation, and he threatened to sell all the female slaves to other plantations. This would mean breaking up all the slave families, which Darwin thought was terribly cruel. By the time Darwin arrived back in Rio, his heart was filled with hatred for the European slaveowners of Brazil. Needless to say, he never mentioned this experience to FitzRoy. More than ever, he realized how right his grandfathers and father had been in opposing slavery.

The *Beagle* was going to sail back up to Bahia to do more scientific measurements, so Darwin stayed behind in Rio. The *Beagle* would return later and pick him up. Along with the ship's artist, he rented a cottage on a beach near Rio and moved in. Here, his life as a naturalist would begin in earnest.

For two months, Darwin spent all day, every day, riding deep into the rainforest to collect specimens. In a single day he collected more species of beetle than he had found during an entire year in England. He developed a new passion for spiders; there were so many bizarre tropical spider species that he could search for years and never find them all. He was still shooting birds just as he had done during hunting season back home, but it was no longer for fun—now it was for science. The taxidermy skills he had learned in Edinburgh came in handy for preserving bird specimens. He wrote letters to Henslow in Cambridge describing his discoveries. Darwin's specimen collection quickly grew enormous. He started hiring young Brazilians to help him collect more and more.

At the end of June 1832, the *Beagle* finally returned to pick him up. Once back aboard, he learned that three crewmen (including Darwin's first friend on the ship) had died of malaria. Furthermore, the ship's doctor, who had been the official naturalist for the journey, had quit (out of jealousy that Darwin was a better collector) and gone back to England on a different ship. Now, at last, Darwin was appointed the official naturalist of the *Beagle*. His collecting was no longer a hobby by any standards. Now it was his sworn *duty* to collect as much as he could.

Young Brazilians brought Darwin many rare specimens he could not have found himself.

Tying the Knot

Even though many of the crewmen aboard the *Beagle* were only teenagers, they were all expert sailors. Up until the 20th century, ships were controlled mainly by means of ropes. Every sailor had to know how to tie dozens of different knots in order to furl and unfurl the sails, manage the rigging, and tie up the ship. One mis-tied knot could mean disaster—a sail coming loose in a storm, or a box of cargo crashing to the deck. Some nautical knots are very complicated, but here are three basic ones that every sailor on the *Beagle* had to master.

What you need
A piece of rope or cord

Using your rope, practice tying these knots:

The Figure-Eight Knot

This knot prevents the end of any rope from slipping through a loop in another rope or through any small hole.

The Figure-Eight Knot

The Bowline

The bowline is used to make a strong loop that will not slip when tension is put on it. The bowline is one of the most common nautical knots, and is used for many purposes, such as raising heavy loads and securing the ship to the dock.

The Bowline

The Sheepshank

The sheepshank is a special knot used to make a rope shorter. It only stays in place if both ends of the rope are pulled tightly. To untie a sheepshank, simply let the rope go slack and the knot will come apart.

The Sheepshank

Adventures in the South

Next, the *Beagle* headed south to the River Plata, which separates Buenos Aires, Argentina, from Montevideo, Uruguay. The climate and landscape changed dramatically. The jungles and rainforest gave way to grasslands and dry plains that got very cold in the winter. The trip was entering a new phase.

For the next two years, the *Beagle* zigzagged back and forth along the coast of Argentina. Down to Tierra del Fuego, back up to Buenos Aires, over to the Falkland Islands, and back to the mainland again, over and over. FitzRoy's job was to make extremely accurate measurements of every aspect of this area, to help the British government create the most accurate maps possible. And the captain was not about to let his country down. He kept checking and double-checking all his measurements, even though it meant sailing through freezing storms for months.

Darwin took advantage of the *Beagle*'s back-tracking by staying on land for long periods of time, arranging to be picked up when the ship returned to the same area. For this reason, this book won't be following the *Beagle*'s movements day by day during the remainder of 1832 and 1833. Instead, it will focus on some important incidents, and follow what happened to Darwin.

The Fossil-Hunter

As the *Beagle* scanned the coastline of Argentina, tracing the exact outline of its shore and taking soundings (measuring how deep the water is), Darwin made an important discovery. One day, while exploring by boat an area called Punta Alta, he noticed what seemed to be a fossil embedded in a cliff face. He landed, and discovered that there was not just one fossil but dozens of them up and down the cliff. He dug some out only to find that they were huge, as big as the bones of an elephant. He brought them back to the ship, and later returned to the area several times to dig out more bones. Darwin was sure they did not come from any kind of animal that still lived in South America. He was positive that they were from species that had gone extinct (died out), yet he could not identify which ones, as he was not yet an expert in paleontology. FitzRoy and the crew were a bit annoyed that Darwin was dragging all this "rubbish" onto the overcrowded *Beagle,* but now that Darwin was the official naturalist there was little they could do about it, aside from nicknaming him "Flycatcher."

Darwin himself was thrilled. In a letter home, he wrote, "I have been wonderfully lucky with fossil bones. Some of the animals must have been of great dimensions." He packed them up to be later shipped back home to Henslow. Because in those days ships often sank and cargo was sometimes stolen, he had no idea for over a year whether or not his packages had even made it safely back to England. He secretly feared that Henslow would laugh at his amateur attempts. He had no idea what a commotion his shipments were causing among the scientists of Europe.

One of the fossilized skeletons was from an extinct giant ground sloth called a *megatherium;* an-

A reconstruction of one of the fossils Darwin found.

A giant ground sloth, with a huge South American armadillo in the background. Both these animals were extinct, but Darwin found fossils that enabled scientists to reconstruct what they looked like.

other was from an extinct armadillo that had been as big as a rhinoceros. Another was from a type of rodent (like a mouse or a rat) as big as an elephant! These finds really started Darwin thinking about how species change over time. Were the modern sloths and armadillos of South America related to these ancient giant ones? At the time most scientists believed that each species was unrelated to all others; that these extinct animals had died out suddenly and were later replaced by new types of animals somehow created by God or nature. But it made more sense to Darwin that the older, larger versions of the animals had slowly become smaller and changed slightly, bit by bit, over time until they looked like the modern animals. He mused for a while over the idea, but he had so much else to do that he decided to wait until he got home to figure this out completely.

A Determined Collector

Even though the *Beagle* eventually spent two years on the eastern coast of South America (much longer than originally planned), Darwin was actually only on board less than one-third of that time. FitzRoy would drop him off and then pick him up later. This way Darwin could do more exploring without getting seasick! After a while he realized he needed help during his excursions. So he hired the ship's fiddler, a teenage boy named Syms Covington, to be his scientific assistant. He taught Covington how to shoot, how to stuff birds, and how to place specimens in bottles. As a result Darwin nearly doubled his productivity. The poor *Beagle* was full to burst-

ing with animal pelts, fossils, bugs in jars and boxes, barrels of fish, stuffed birds, and boxes of rocks and minerals. At every opportunity Darwin sent as many items as he could back to England, but the ship's storage area would again quickly fill up.

Often he would go out on the *pampas,* the wide-open grasslands of southern Argentina. The South American cowboys, called *gauchos,* would ride with him and teach him how to live off the land. He hunted rheas (South American ostriches), ate beside campfires, and sang songs in Spanish with mustachioed bandits. He even discovered a new kind of rhea that was later named after him. The spoiled English schoolboy had grown into a seasoned world traveler.

Despite Darwin's freewheeling adventures, the political situation in South America was very dangerous. More than once he found himself caught up in the middle of revolutions: warlords, soldiers, looters, and Indians shooting at each other every which way. During one incident, he and Covington fled Buenos Aires on the very last boat out of town as bullets whizzed overhead.

After a year of silence, Darwin finally received a letter from Henslow. What news! Not only had all of Darwin's shipments arrived, but Henslow had shown them to the top scientists in England. They were astounded by the fossils. Henslow had taken the letters Darwin had written to him and presented them to the leading scientific societies as if they were official research documents. Everyone is talking about you, Henslow wrote. When you return, you'll be one of the most respected scientists in England!

Darwin was ecstatic. Suddenly the seasickness, exhausting excursions, danger, and long, boring waits all seemed worth it. If he had ever considered quitting, that thought was set aside forever. Henceforth, he was a scientist.

The Civilized Savages

One of the *Beagle*'s goals had nothing to do with surveying coastlines or making scientific measurements. It had to do with spreading European civilization. In 1830, on the previous trip that FitzRoy had taken to Tierra del Fuego at the southernmost tip of the continent (before Darwin had joined the crew), he had come into conflict with the local In-

dians, a very primitive tribe called the Fuegians. After some of the tribesmen had stolen one of FitzRoy's smaller boats, he had taken some of the Indians hostage, hoping to trade them for the boat. The plan didn't work, and most of the captives escaped. One little girl, however, wanted to stay on the *Beagle.* The crew named her Fuegia Basket. FitzRoy, who was deeply convinced of his duty to bring European-style civilization to the far corners of the world, was inspired to hatch a grand scheme. He brought three more Fuegians on board and without warning sailed away, eventually bringing them all back to England.

His plan was to "civilize" the four kidnapped Fuegians, and then return them to their native land, where they in turn would civilize their entire tribe. One of the Fuegians died of smallpox

Darwin discovered this rare species of rhea. It was later named *Rhea darwini* after him.

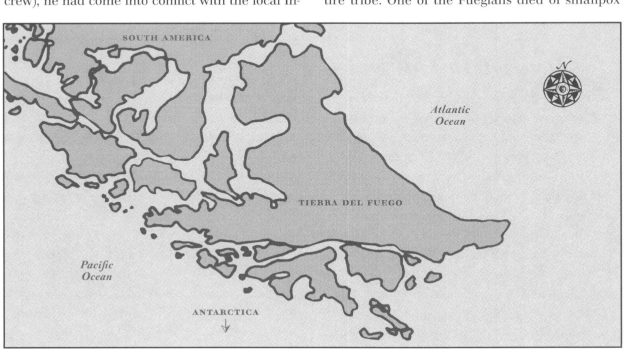

Tierra del Fuego, at the southern tip of South America.

Portraits of the three Fuegians. Top row: Fuegia Basket as she looked in England, and then as she looked back home in Tierra del Fuego. Middle row: Jemmy Button first as he looked at home, and then dressed as an Englishman. Bottom row: two views of York Minster dressed in European clothes.

shortly after arriving in England, but the remaining three—Fuegia Basket, who was about 9 years old; Jemmy Button, about 16; and York Minster, in his 20s—survived and thrived. They were all taught English, shown how to wear clothes (the Fuegians generally went around naked), baptized as Christians, and instructed in proper British etiquette. Missionary societies, whose goal was to convert the whole world to Christianity, were very excited by FitzRoy's plan. Their members donated boxloads of expensive upper-class housewares—wine glasses, tea trays, soup tureens, tablecloths, and much more—thinking that having such things would somehow help the Fuegians act more English.

So, along with a young missionary named Richard Matthews, the three Fuegians had been aboard the *Beagle* during the entire return trip. On January 23, 1833, the *Beagle* finally landed once again on Fuegia Basket's home island, on a protected beach called Woolya Cove. The three Fuegians—still dressed in proper British clothing, with stiff shirts, high collars, and shiny shoes—went ashore after having been away for three years. The natives who came to meet them watched in amazement as the *Beagle*'s crewmen spent days building huts and a garden for the missionary and his three followers. Matthews was a bit nervous, as he had been told that Fuegians were sometimes friendly but sometimes not. Not knowing what to expect, he waved goodbye to the *Beagle* as it continued its measurements along the coast.

After nine days, the *Beagle* returned to see how things were going at the mission. Darwin was shocked at what they found. From the minute the

Beagle had disappeared from sight, the native Fuegians had attacked the huts, intent on stealing all the cargo. Matthews had fended them off for a few days, but eventually he couldn't hold out any longer. The *Beagle* returned to find all the wine glasses and other expensive items gone, the huts ruined, and a desperate, starving Matthews begging to be brought back on board. After only nine days, the entire mission was in ruins. FitzRoy, as usual, was furious with the Fuegians, whom he now considered to be savages who had no chance of becoming civilized. He and the *Beagle* left Fuegia, Jemmy, and York behind to start their lives all over again. The ship sailed off to continue its explorations elsewhere.

A year later, the *Beagle* was finally done surveying the east coast of South America and had to pass Tierra del Fuego one more time on its way to Chile. FitzRoy decided to drop anchor and see how the Fuegians were doing. To Darwin's astonishment, nothing was left of their experiment in civilization. Jemmy Button rowed out to the ship in a canoe. He was completely naked and covered in dirt, his hair long and uncombed. He had with him a young girl whom he had gotten pregnant. He told the Englishmen that York Minster and Fuegia Basket had stolen all of Jemmy's clothes and remaining possessions. Then York and Fuegia had gotten "married" and moved to a different island. Even though she was only 12 or 13 years old by that time, Fuegia probably already had her own baby. Only Jemmy still remembered any English; the other two had almost immediately gone back to speaking their native language. FitzRoy's experiment, it seemed, had failed completely.

The *Beagle* as it sailed through the Straits of Magellan in
Tierra del Fuego.

Into the Pacific

Darwin found fossilized seashells like these high up in the Andes, proving the mountains had long ago been underwater.

The crew was ecstatic as the *Beagle* finally entered the Pacific Ocean on June 10, 1834. At last! They had spent two years going in circles on the Atlantic side of the continent. Now they sailed up the Pacific coast of Chile and arrived at the big, sophisticated city of Valparaiso, where wealthy European settlers had created a kind of South American Paris. The *Beagle* was to spend some time in port, so Darwin went to stay with a childhood friend named Richard Corfield, who had moved from Shrewsbury to Valparaiso. How strange that these two friends should meet, after so many years, on the other side of the world!

In August, Darwin left Corfield's estate and went on a long excursion to examine the geology of the Andes, a tremendous mountain range which extends all the way along the west coast of South America. For over a month he traipsed about the Andean foothills, chipping away at rocks by day, often staying at the *haciendas* (estates) of wealthy landowners at night. He discovered fossilized seashells thousands of feet above sea level, which further confirmed Lyell's theory that mountain ranges are raised up from the sea floor by slow-moving but unstoppable geologic forces.

Darwin was also strongly attracted to other "beauties of nature" in Chile. He frequently described in his diary the charms of the nation's "pretty signoritas," the smartly dressed, lovely young Spanish ladies he met during his travels.

He had no time for romance, however. In September he got terribly sick from drinking some sour wine and had to be carried back to Corfield's home. Poor Darwin spent a month in bed with agonizing stomach problems. Historians have speculated that the stomach pains he experienced later in life may have been related to this episode.

Darwin wasn't the only person to fall sick that September. Captain FitzRoy also had a breakdown, but his had nothing to do with his stomach. It was a mental breakdown. Earlier in the journey, FitzRoy had purchased some small schooners to help with the *Beagle*'s measurements. But he had not first asked for permission from the Admiralty, the part of the British government that controlled seafaring. He had used his own money to buy the schooners, then asked the government to pay him back. At Valparaiso, he finally received his answer: the Admiralty refused to pay him back and even scolded him for acting against orders. FitzRoy was always unstable and on edge, but this time he finally snapped. How dare they criticize him! Furthermore, he was completely broke, and now had to sell the schooners. FitzRoy stomped about in a rage, and then announced, "I quit! The expedition is over!" He feared that he was going insane.

Word got back to Darwin in his sickbed. He worried how he would ever get home. But as the weeks passed, FitzRoy's "Hot Coffee" temper cooled down. The ship's officers convinced him that they all had to get back to England anyway, so why not just take the *Beagle*? And since we're all going back aboard the *Beagle*, why not just spend a little more time finishing the survey?

FitzRoy, as was his habit, changed his mind.

He announced he wasn't really quitting and then apologized to everyone. The voyage would continue. In November, Darwin was feeling better and joined the *Beagle* as it headed back south to take measurements along the coast of Chile. One night during this survey, Darwin and the crew saw a volcano erupting in the distance, which Darwin eagerly watched through a telescope.

Earth in Upheaval

In February 1835, having completed the survey of southern Chile, the *Beagle* stayed for a while at the port city of Valdivia. On February 20, Darwin was out in the woods as usual, hunting for insects, when he lay down on the ground for a rest. Suddenly, the earth started to tremble. He tried to stand up, but his knees buckled and he was knocked back down. For two solid minutes the entire landscape shook violently. Darwin had just experienced his first earthquake. He rushed back into town and saw that many of the wooden buildings had been damaged. FitzRoy ordered all hands back on board and the ship quickly sailed up the coast to Concepción, a major port. They arrived to find the city in ruins. Most of the buildings in Concepción were made of stone, and stone houses usually crumble in earthquakes. A town official rushed up to tell them that "not a house in Concepción is standing…seventy villages were destroyed." Furthermore, a huge *tsunami* (a massive ocean wave caused by an earthquake) had washed away all the buildings near the shore. Darwin went to inspect the coast and reported that the entire shoreline for

miles was "strewn over with timber and furniture, as if a thousand great ships had been wrecked. Besides chairs, tables, and bookshelves in great numbers, there were several roofs of cottages, which had drifted in an almost entire state." (Exactly 125 years later, in 1960, Valdivia was the epicenter of the largest earthquake in recorded history: 9.5 on the Richter Scale. No one knows how strong the 1835 quake was, but from Darwin's description it may have been just as powerful.)

While the *Beagle* aided in the recovery efforts, Darwin discovered that whole sections of land had risen several feet straight out of the sea during the quake, and stayed in place. He saw clusters of mussels attached to rocks that had once been underwater, now dead and rotting far above the shoreline. Here was the most direct proof of all, he wrote, of Lyell's geological theories. Darwin had seen with his own eyes the land rising out of the sea little by little. After millions more years and thousands more earthquakes, those mussels he saw would become fossilized shells at the top of the Andes.

Darwin wanted to confirm it once and for all. The *Beagle* docked again in Valparaiso to take on new supplies and prepare for the long journey across the Pacific, so Darwin decided he had time to climb up to the top of the Andes (earlier, he had only reached the foothills). Using Richard Corfield's house as a base yet again, he set off with native guides on his longest excursion yet. They climbed and climbed all the way to the highest pass in the mountain range. Sure enough, just as he had predicted, at the top he found fossilized seashells embedded in the rock. He now knew for sure that the

South American Comida

While in Chile, Darwin often dined in the *haciendas* (large estates or ranches) of Spanish-speaking colonists. There he tasted for the first time some of the delicious cuisine native to this part of Latin America—a far cry from what he was used to eating back in England and on board the *Beagle*. This classic Chilean dish uses local ingredients and is based on a 19th-century recipe. It is more than likely that Darwin enjoyed this dish many times, as it was (and still remains) a standard meal in many Chilean homes:

Porotos Granados

What you need

2 cups (480 ml) fresh or dried cranberry
    beans

3 tablespoons (45 ml) olive oil

1 tablespoon (15 ml) paprika

2 medium onions, coarsely chopped

3 fresh chopped tomatoes, or one 14-oz. can
    of diced tomatoes

1 teaspoon (5 ml) basil

½ teaspoon (2.5 ml) oregano

Salt and chili powder to taste

2½ cups (600 ml), or 1 pound (450 g) squash,
    cut into 1-inch (2.5-cm) cubes

1¼ cups (300 ml) fresh or frozen corn kernels

Notes: Cranberry beans are not cranberries but rather a delicious kind of bean also sometimes called borlotti beans, Roman beans, fagiolo romano, or other names. They are white with reddish speckles. If you can't find them, you can use Great Northern beans, cannellini beans, lima beans, or pinto beans instead. Try to use fresh or dried beans instead of canned beans.

The best kinds of squash to use are winter squash, butternut squash, banana squash, acorn squash, or pumpkin. Remember to remove the outer skin of the squash.

The measurements need not be precise. Use more or less of any ingredient as you wish.

If using dried beans, place them in large pot half filled with cold water. Bring to a boil, turn off the heat and let the beans soak for an hour. Drain the old water, add fresh water, bring the beans to a boil again, reduce the heat, and simmer for another hour. If using fresh beans, wash them first and put them into a large pot half filled with water. Bring to a boil, lower the heat, and simmer about 45 minutes until the beans are tender. Drain off the water, saving some for later.

In a frying pan, heat the oil and the paprika together. Stir in the chopped onion and sauté until the onion is sweet. Add the tomatoes, basil, oregano, and salt, and simmer them all together. Stir frequently on low heat for about 10 minutes or until the mixture is well blended. Add water if necessary. Combine this mixture, the squash, and the beans in the large pot. Add some of the set-aside water, stir, and simmer on low heat for 15 minutes. The squash will disintegrate and create a thick sauce. Add in the corn and simmer for 5 more minutes or until the beans and corn are both tender. Add extra salt or chili powder if desired. Serve in shallow bowls.

Earth was millions of years old, if not older. Nothing else could explain what he observed in Chile.

On the way back down the Andes he discovered something even more unusual: a forest of petrified trees, which he took as further proof of the Earth's age and the massive geological shifts which must have caused the trees to become fossilized. He got back to Corfield's house in early April and sent another immense shipment of specimens to Henslow, as well as a letter describing all his new discoveries.

He eventually rejoined the *Beagle* on July 6 and sailed north to Peru. It was supposed to be a short stop before heading out into the Pacific, but yet another revolution kept the ship and its passengers from departing. Finally they escaped and left South America behind. On September 15 they reached their first stop in the Pacific: the Galapagos Islands.

The Galapagos

Much has been written about Darwin's visit to the Galapagos. When most people hear the islands' name, the first thing they think is, *"That's the place where Darwin discovered evolution, isn't it?"* They think the whole purpose of the *Beagle*'s journey was to visit the Galapagos. In truth, however, the Galapagos were a rather unimportant stopover on the journey, for both the *Beagle* and Darwin. He *was* looking forward to visiting these strange islands 600 miles off the coast of Ecuador, but it was their geology he wanted to investigate, not their wildlife.

It was only much later, back in England, that Darwin realized how important his visit had been.

His first impressions of the Galapagos were not good:

The black lava rocks on the beach are frequented by large (2 to 3 feet) most disgusting clumsy lizards.... When on shore I proceeded to botanize and obtained ten different flowers; but such insignificant, ugly little flowers, as would better become an arctic than a tropical country.

The sun beat down relentlessly, the black lava was too hot to walk on, and aside from a few reptiles and birds, there were hardly any animals—a small number of insects, and no mammals. Some misinformation also dampened any enthusiasm Darwin might have had; he was told that the famed giant Galapagos tortoises had been imported from the Indian Ocean. Since the Galapagos were not their native habitat, he thought, there was little reason to study the tortoises. He had also learned, incorrectly, that the marine iguanas—the only lizards in the world that swim in the ocean—were imports from South America and not particularly unique. And the birds were mostly just plain brown and black finches, very common and not especially interesting.

To Darwin, the most fascinating aspect of the animals on the Galapagos was how strangely tame they were. Once Darwin walked right up to a hawk perched on a branch and gently knocked it off. The bird made no attempt to fly away. Darwin then

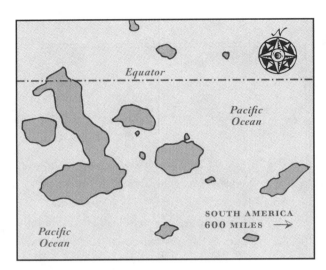

The Galapagos Islands.

climbed onto a giant tortoise and rode it as if it were a horse; it just walked along, stopping for a drink, as if he wasn't even there. The crew dragged 18 of the tortoises onto the *Beagle* to serve as food for the upcoming voyage—a common practice for any ship visiting the Galapagos in those days.

Darwin spent many days collecting what samples he could, but in truth he did not go to any more effort than he had done during any of his other excursions. Thinking that all the birds were the same on each of the different islands, he absentmindedly neglected to properly identify which specimen came from which island—a thoughtless mistake that he would later regret.

The geology of the islands was indeed strange. Darwin inspected fields of mini-volcanoes which in the past had been the source of the island's lava—lava which had cooled down so recently that it was as hard as iron. Not enough time had passed since the islands first emerged from the sea for

The only three large species native to the Galapagos: land iguanas (top), marine iguanas (center), and giant tortoises (right).

soil to accumulate on top of the hardened rock. As a result, little could grow there except cactus, which the tortoises and land iguanas ate. With not much else to eat on land, the marine iguanas had taken to eating the seaweed found offshore. The birds pecked at the seeds dropped by a smattering of weeds and wildflowers.

The only human inhabitants on the Galapagos were the inmates of a prison colony on Charles Island (now called Isla Santa Maria). The governor of the colony mentioned to Darwin that he could tell which island a particular tortoise came from simply by looking at the patterns on its shell. It was

that offhand comment that started a long, slow chain reaction in Darwin's mind that eventually led him to some of his greatest insights.

Belatedly, Darwin began to notice that the birds on each of the islands also differed in appearance, depending on where they came from. He was able to start properly labeling some of his specimens, but he wrote in his diary, regretfully:

I never dreamed that islands, about fifty or sixty miles apart, and most of them in sight of each other, formed of precisely the same rocks, placed under a quite similar climate, rising to

Darwin walking with a giant tortoise.

Galapagos giant tortoises. The designs of their shells varied island by island. Notice the two Galapagos finches at the bottom of the picture.

What's So Special About the Galapagos?

Most people know that Darwin visited the Galapagos Islands, but very few understand what made them so significant in Darwin's thinking about evolution. The key lies in two concepts: *similarities* and *differences*.

Similarities

The birds on the Galapagos, Darwin knew, were quite similar to the ones on the South American mainland, 600 miles (960 km) away. It's logical to assume that the two populations are related to each other, that some long-ago birds from South America flew or hitched a ride out to the islands and started a new colony there. The same process goes on all the time with other animals all over the world.

Differences

But upon closer inspection Darwin learned that the Galapagos birds are slightly but noticeably different from their South American cousins. More importantly, the birds on each of the different islands were *not* identical. Some had small beaks for picking up the tiny seeds native to one island. Some had narrow beaks for probing small holes on another island. Some had big beaks for breaking open the large, tough seeds that grew on yet another island. Ornithologists (bird experts) confirmed that each island had its own species of birds, even though they might all look quite similar at first glance.

What did this mean? The common theory at the time was that each species had been separately created by God at the time of Genesis. But, Darwin reasoned, didn't it make much more sense that a small group of birds had migrated to the Galapagos from South America long ago, and that over many generations the birds on each island had adapted to survive in their particular ecosystem? That they had *evolved* from the same ancestors to assume these different shapes and eventually grew apart to such an extent that they became different species? A slightly different ecosystem on each island (different sizes of seeds) had compelled each population to adapt in different ways (different sizes of beaks).

Because the Galapagos are so isolated, they work as a sort of test case. There are very few species there, and very little contact with other ecosystems. Darwin realized that if this principle was true for the birds of the Galapagos, it was true for every animal in every ecosystem in the world, and that all the species we see today evolved from earlier species—and were not created all at the same time by a creator.

a nearly equal height, would have been differently tenanted.... It is the fate of most voyagers, no sooner to discover what is most interesting in any locality, than they are hurried from it; but I ought, perhaps to be thankful that I obtained sufficient materials to establish this most remarkable fact in the distribution of organic beings.

But there was no time to think about all that now. On October 20, 1835, FitzRoy declared, Raise the anchors! We're off across the Pacific, on our way home at last.

Homeward Bound

Though the final year of the voyage took them most of the way around the globe, past many of the most exotic locations in the world, Darwin paid them little mind. Like the rest of the crew, he just wanted to go home.

With the wind at their backs, they sailed across the entire Pacific Ocean with amazing speed, arriving at Tahiti after only three weeks. The ship only stayed there for a short time, yet Darwin greatly enjoyed it nonetheless. He marveled at the delicious bananas, pineapples, guavas, coconuts, and breadfruit growing wild all over the island. He was also puzzled by the extreme differences he perceived between the native Tahitians and the Fuegians. Although both tribes were equally "primitive" by European standards, he saw the Fuegians as

dishonest, ignorant, ugly, and incapable of improvement, while the Tahitians seemed friendly, generous, attractive, intelligent, and improving every day. Many of them had become Christians, which he saw as a good thing.

The next stop was New Zealand. On the way there Darwin pondered the coral reefs found throughout the Pacific. No one had yet figured out exactly how coral reefs were created. Darwin knew that the reefs—which look like outcroppings of bumpy orange or pink stone—were built up slowly by tiny animals that created the coral as a protective covering. The animals could only live in shallow warm water, yet the reefs sometimes extended far, far down to the deep ocean floor. Also, sometimes the reefs surrounded an island, but other times they just grew in a circle with no island at all in the middle, a formation called an *atoll*. Lyell's theory, which most people accepted, was that the reefs grew on the lips of volcanic craters that were underwater. This, Lyell wrote, explained why the reefs were usually circular. But Darwin felt that this time Lyell had it all wrong. If the land was rising in the Andes, at one end of the Pacific, then it was probably sinking at the other end. Darwin suspected that the coral reefs would start to grow in the shallow water around the perimeter of an island. After thousands and thousands of years, the island would start to sink, and the reefs would grow upward to keep their top layers, which contained the living coral, just under the surface where the water was warm. The dead, hardened part of the coral remained in the lower layers. Sometimes, the island would sink entirely out of sight, but the

Voyage Journal

Darwin took lots of notes during his sea voyage and later wrote a popular book about his adventure. You too can write your own *Voyage of the Beagle.*

What you need
A blank book or writing pad
A pen or pencil

The next time you take a trip out of town, either on a day-trip or a longer vacation, write down in your journal everything that happens to you. (If you aren't planning a trip anytime soon, describe a day traveling around your town.) You can either note your thoughts and observations right as they happen, or pause to write a few times during the day, or wait until evening, and then write down the whole day's events. Describe the scenery, any out-of-the-ordinary sights, conversations you overhear, and anything else you think noteworthy. Pay attention to details. Try to notice tiny things you normally wouldn't notice.

When you get back home, add any extra details you remember. Then give your journal an old-fashioned title, such as *My Travels to the Mountains and What I Saw There.*

reefs would keep growing and growing to maintain their position at the water's surface. This would explain the presence of atolls throughout the South Pacific, as well as the reefs that extended far down to the deep ocean floor—a floor that had once been much higher. Luckily for Darwin, FitzRoy's final assignment was to investigate some coral reefs in the Indian Ocean, so the theory could be investigated.

The *Beagle* made only a short stop in New Zealand. Darwin had little time for collecting, so he merely strolled around to see what the place was like. He didn't have a very high opinion of the Maori, the native people of New Zealand. Though closely related to the Tahitians, they were ferocious warriors and reputed to be cannibals. Many of the white settlers were ex-convicts and lawless drunkards, and they made an even worse impression on Darwin than the Maori did. In Darwin's eyes, the British missionaries, very prim and proper and pious, seemed to be the only good thing about New Zealand.

Darwin was surprised at how much he liked the missionaries in both Tahiti and New Zealand. Before the voyage, back in England, he had believed that missionaries were cruel conquerors who wanted to wipe out native cultures and replace them with English culture. So he fully expected to hate the missionaries. But deep in his heart he was still an upper-class Englishman who had, after all, studied to be a clergyman. The native cultures he saw during his voyage usually seemed violent and chaotic, so he came to feel that a Christianized country was a more peaceful country, which made everyone happier—natives and colonists alike. Darwin would have been amazed to learn that, almost 200 years later, people would still be arguing over whether colonization was good or terrible.

From New Zealand the *Beagle* made the short hop to Sydney, Australia. Darwin was at first impressed—and soon after disgusted—by the rowdy boomtown, populated mostly by criminals who had been exiled from England. Despite being part of a penal colony—a vast prison as big as a continent—Sydney was bursting with wealthy ex-convicts who had become merchants making fortunes exporting wool from Australian sheep all over the world. But the place offered very little mental stimulation for a curious man like Charles Darwin. His excursion inland was also disappointing, as the sheep ranchers had killed off most of the native wildlife.

The *Beagle* left Australia after a few more stops and reached the Keeling (now called Cocos) Islands in the Indian Ocean on April 1, 1836. These extremely isolated islets (small islands) are composed entirely of coral, on which nothing but coconut trees grow. Darwin spent days wading through the shallow water, marveling at the tropical fish, picking up samples of living corals, and lying on the beach sipping coconut juice. He peered at the coral organisms through his microscope. He was unable to resolve the mystery of whether corals were plants or animals; no one knew yet. But, thanks to his observations and FitzRoy's measurements of coral reefs that extended downward thousands of feet, Darwin was convinced that his theory of reefs growing on sinking islands was correct.

After the Keeling Islands, there was nothing left for the *Beagle* to do but sail home. On the way, FitzRoy was supposed to continue taking measurements of longitude, using a vast collection of chronometers (precise clocks) he had brought along for that very purpose. The *Beagle* crossed the Indian Ocean and made a quick stop in South Africa. At Ascension Island, Darwin found some more mail awaiting him. His sister Catherine had written that Henslow had turned several of Darwin's scientific letters into a booklet and printed many copies—without asking Darwin's permission! Top scientists and gentlemen were reading the booklets, and Darwin was the talk of the town. Darwin was simultaneously proud and embarrassed; he had written his letters thinking only Henslow would read them.

A colony of living coral animals.

After South Africa, FitzRoy had surprising news for those aboard the *Beagle:* he announced that they had to return to Brazil one last time, to complete their official circumnavigation of the globe and confirm that his longitude measurements all matched. Of course, they didn't really *need* to; FitzRoy was just a perfectionist. Everyone was extremely unhappy, yet they had to obey. It was impossible to argue with the captain. Darwin by now had completely run out of patience. He wrote, "This zig-zagging manner of proceeding is very grievous; it has put the finishing stroke to my feelings. I loathe, I abhor the sea."

After another short stay in Brazil, and more delays due to bad weather, the *Beagle* headed straight north toward England. The entire ship was bursting with anticipation. Nearly five years had passed since the men had been home. Darwin lay awake at night, swinging in his hammock, imagining the carriages he would take to Shrewsbury. What had changed? Would anything be the way it used to be? He didn't realize that it was *he* who had changed. No longer a fun-loving "varmint," he had matured into a determined and serious scientist. His ocean journey may have been over, but his journey of the mind was just beginning.

During the stormy night of October 2, 1836, the shore of England appeared through the clouds. After four years, nine months, and five days at sea, the *Beagle* pulled into the southern port of Falmouth. Charles Darwin had been around the globe and had seen sights no one had ever seen. But the cold, wet soil of his homeland was to him the sweetest vision in the world. Home at last!

4

The Search for Reasons

A Journey of the Mind

Returning from his *Beagle* adventure, Darwin had no time to relax. So much to do, so many scientific questions left unanswered! He later said that the two years after his voyage were the busiest of his whole life.

He rushed back to Shrewsbury by carriage, but arrived at The Mount after everyone was already asleep. So, as a joke, he tiptoed into his bedroom, got a good night's rest, and strolled into breakfast the next morning as if he had never been gone at all. Everyone leaped from their chairs. Charles was back! His sisters kissed him and laughed and cried, and even the servants celebrated. He wrote a letter to Henslow saying he was "giddy with joy and confusion."

He hardly knew where to start. After his happy family reunion, he dashed back to Cambridge, where he stayed with Henslow. What was he to do with all the shipments he had sent back, and the thousands more specimens still waiting to be unloaded from the *Beagle*? They needed to be classified, catalogued, and studied. It was all far too much for Charles to do himself. How could he make sense of this jumble of boxes and bottles? With Henslow's help he arranged to have leading experts in each field take parts of the collection. Richard Owen, a famous animal anatomist, examined the fossils. A highly respected ornithologist named John Gould agreed to examine the birds. Others got the lizards, the insects, and the shells.

Darwin finally got everything off the *Beagle* and rented a room in Cambridge to sort it all out. FitzRoy was writing an official account of the voyage and asked Darwin to write a special companion volume about his natural history discoveries. Darwin gathered all his notes and spent most of

People in Victorian England flocked to see fossils displayed in museums.

the next year putting together the book we now know as *The Voyage of the* Beagle.

The problem was, most of the leading scientists Darwin needed to consult lived in London. He trav-eled there many times, staying with his brother Erasmus. He met his idol Charles Lyell, the man whose book had so inspired him on his journeys. Darwin was nervous, not knowing what he would say to such a great man, but to his surprise it was Lyell who treated Darwin like a celebrity, thanking him over and over for confirming the theories in Lyell's book. They ended up being great friends.

Darwin couldn't impose on his brother forever, so in March 1837 he rented his own place in what he called "dirty, odious London." The city was filled with coal-burning factories and smoke-billowing chimneys. The smog and pollution were so bad that even on a sunny day the air was thick with black soot that made breathing difficult and gave poor Darwin headaches. If he was to make his mark as a scientist, however, he had no choice but to live in the filthy metropolis.

The anatomist Richard Owen, next to a skeleton he reconstructed.

Charles Lyell.

Mystery of the Finches

Once there, he heard from Gould, the ornithologist. Gould told him that the bird specimens Darwin had brought back from the Galapagos were all mis-labeled. Judging from their differently shaped beaks, Darwin thought he had brought back a var-ied collection of blackbirds, wrens, warblers, and finches. Gould told him that in fact they were *all* finches, each one a separate species no one had ever identified before. A separate collection of mock-ingbirds was also a new discovery unknown to sci-ence—each mockingbird was a distinct species. Both the finches and the mockingbirds were related to other species from South America.

Galapagos finches had already inspired Darwin to start focusing more closely on what he called the "transmutation of species," the slow changing of one species into another, which today is called evolution. (Despite the fact that Darwin is known as the founder of the science of evolution, the word "evolution" was rarely used in his lifetime. He preferred the terms "transmutation" or "descent with modification," and in the first edition of *Origin of Species* he never used the word "evolution.")

After talking with Gould, Darwin pondered for a long time. A flock of finches, he felt, must have long ago been blown by a storm from the South American mainland out to the Galapagos. Some landed on one island, some landed on other islands. But each island was unique, with a slightly different selection of seeds to eat. Over time, with every succeeding generation, each group of finches—now isolated on different islands—slowly acquired different beak shapes best suited to eating what was available. The finches convinced him that this "transmutation" *must* have occurred, yet he still couldn't quite figure out what caused the change.

A modern armadillo.

Seeds of a New Idea

His feelings were confirmed by the findings of Owen, who announced that Darwin's fossils were indeed from gigantic versions of animals similar to smaller ones that still lived in South America. One looked like a huge armadillo, another like a giant llama, another a massive sloth, and yet another was an immense rodent. Armadillos, llamas, sloths, and rodents all still lived in South America, but the modern animals were much smaller. Since none of the giant animals could be found alive anywhere, it was obvious that they had all become extinct. How logical was it, Darwin mused, that they had all died out, and then a whole *new* group of animals that looked quite similar but which were *completely unrelated* somehow magically appeared? It seemed obvious that over time the race of giant armadillos had become smaller and smaller until they eventually looked like modern armadillos. In other words, the fossils were the ancestors of the animals we see today.

Darwin found the fossils of this extinct giant armadillo.

Make Your Own Fossils

Darwin wasn't the only person of his era fascinated by fossils. A "fossil craze" spread all across Europe in the middle of the 19th century, and amateur fossil-hunters searched for them everywhere. Despite the intense interest, however, there was great disagreement as to whether fossils were the remains of ancient animals or simply pretty designs in the rock that occurred naturally. Scientists eventually proved that fossils were once animals and plants whose remains were "mineralized" over many centuries. But you don't have to wait a million years to make your own fossil. Here's how you can create one in an hour.

Fossils cropped up everywhere in people's imaginations. This old cartoon shows a child riding a rocking-fossil.

What you need
clay or Play-Doh
chicken bones, twigs, seashells, acorns, or toy animals
plaster of Paris or Elmer's Glue
felt pens or watercolor paints (optional)

Place a few handfuls of the clay or Play-Doh into a shallow bowl. (If you don't have any clay at home, you can make some of your own by mixing spoonfuls of water and salt into a bowl of flour, adding a little bit at a time and kneading it until it is the right consistency.) Make sure the clay is at least two inches (5 cm) deep.

Take either a chicken bone (left over from dinner), a small twig, a seashell, an acorn, or a small toy animal and press it into the clay until only the top half remains visible. Remove your object as carefully as you can (you may need to use tweezers or pliers if your object is small), making sure to leave a clear "impression" in the clay.

Then mix a small amount of plaster of Paris according to the instructions on the box, and with a spoon carefully pour it into your mold until it is full. (If you don't have plaster of Paris, you can use Elmer's Glue instead, though it takes longer to harden.)

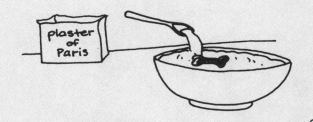

Wait until the plaster or glue has hardened. It will take as little as half an hour for small molds to overnight for very big ones. Carefully "excavate" your fossil by digging out the clay around it until the plaster or hardened glue comes free. Remove any remaining bits of clay and behold—you now have an exact copy of the original object.

If you want it to look more like a fossil (the plaster is white when it dries), color your object with brown or gray watercolor paints or with a wide felt pen. You can repeat the process with other objects and make several different shapes of "fossils."

But this idea, as self-evident as it may seem now, was considered shocking—almost blasphemous—in 1837. Most Britons thought the Bible was literally true, and it said that God created the animals all at once. Nothing more need be said. Yes, there were a few thinkers who suggested exactly what Darwin was pondering, but they were considered radicals or revolutionaries. Darwin hated controversy and did not want to cause a fuss. Yet he couldn't deny the evidence right before his eyes. So, instead of telling anyone about his thoughts, in July 1837 he started a secret notebook. He wrote in his diary,

In July opened first note-book on Transmutation of Species. Had been greatly struck from about the month of previous March on character of South American fossils, and species on Galapagos Archipelago. These facts (especially latter), origin of all my views.

He knew even then that he was going to be doing a lot of thinking on the topic, and he wanted to keep all his thoughts organized in one place.

Darwin knew very well that his ideas didn't match people's religious feelings. But during this time he also was coming to see that the Bible shouldn't be regarded as a science textbook. All throughout the *Beagle* voyage, the sailors had joked that Darwin quoted from the Bible as the answer to any difficulty. Three years in divinity school had made him quite the biblical scholar, even if he

A Bible illustration showing God creating the animals.

of his time was spent writing his book about the voyage of the *Beagle.* It was eventually published in 1839 as one volume of a three-volume series about the journey. The other two volumes, written by FitzRoy and a man named King, were boring and hard to read. But everyone liked Darwin's contribution—so much that a few years later it was published as a separate book called *Journal of Researches into the Natural History and Geology of the Countries Visited During the Voyage of H.M.S.* Beagle *Round the World: Under the Command of Capt. FitzRoy.* With a title like that, you can see why most people just refer to it as *The Voyage of the* Beagle. He had so much material that he also started two separate books, one just about the voyage's zoology (animals) and another just about the geology (rocks).

Living among all the married gentlemen of London forced Darwin to confront a topic he had never really thought about before: should he get married? After all, he was already 29 years old, and aside from Fanny he had never even had a girlfriend. In typical Darwin fashion he sat down and made a list of reasons why he should or should not get married. Having a wife was a "terrible loss of time" that would turn him into an "indolent, idle fool," but a wife was "better than a dog anyhow." Looking over his list, he decided, rather emotionlessly, that the time had come for him to get married after all.

But to whom? Such a troublesome question hadn't occurred to him. By chance, that summer his cousin Emma Wedgwood visited Eras in London, and Darwin took note of her yet again. So many Darwins and Wedgwoods had married each

hadn't been the best student. But now, in 1837 and 1838, he realized that the new scientific knowledge was in direct conflict with *biblical literalism,* or the idea that every word in the Bible was literally true. So, a bit reluctantly, he slowly gave up his belief in the Bible as a historical or scientific document. It was an important book of wise and wonderful moral truths, he felt, but something that should be put aside when dealing with science.

Life and Love in London

His friendship with Lyell grew and Darwin often went to dinner parties with him or with Eras, which was his brother Erasmus's new nickname. But most

Emma Wedgwood Darwin.

other over the years that choosing Emma seemed almost like a family tradition. Besides, she *was* quite pretty, and had quite a bit of money as well. Was he in love? Not yet, perhaps, but surely they could grow to love each other. He made his decision and that fall he proposed. Half-wondering what had taken him so long, Emma accepted right away.

Malthus and Mother Nature

It was right around this time, in October 1838, that Darwin read Thomas Malthus's *Essay on the Principle of Population.* In it, Malthus discussed the notion of universal overpopulation, or the fact that every animal mother, over her lifetime, gives birth to far more offspring than can survive. If they all survived, Malthus wrote, the whole planet would soon be completely covered in animals. So, in the harsh world of nature, most young animals die one way or another before they reach maturity. Darwin realized that the ones who stay alive must, on average, be slightly better equipped to survive than their fellow animals. A cheetah chasing a herd of antelopes will catch the slowest one. The remaining antelopes will run away and survive long enough to have baby antelopes of their own—babies that will inherit their parents' fast legs. This is how antelopes have evolved to run quickly, since slow antelopes have rarely lived long enough to have slow babies.

This was the key that Darwin had been searching for. He was already convinced that the "trans-mutation of species" occurred. And now, with the help of Malthus, for the first time he could see *how* it occurred. Given enough time, these little changes could grow and grow until a new species would emerge from the old one.

Darwin had long been fascinated by professional animal breeders. They would breed the fattest pigs, strongest horses, most docile cats, or fastest dogs by choosing the animals in each generation with the traits they wanted, and having these animals mate. Their offspring were even fatter, stronger, more docile, or faster on average than the previous generation. The breeders kept repeating the process until whole new types of pigs, horses, dogs, or cats evolved over time. (All the different breeds of dogs existing today—from Chihuahuas to Saint Bernards to greyhounds—were created this way!) The process for making new breeds, guided by the hand of man, is called *artificial selection.* Darwin could see that the mechanism he proposed for transmutation was exactly the same, but without the interference of man. Nature did the selecting. So he dubbed his new concept *natural selection.*

The Family Man Takes Ill

Darwin continued working on his specialty books about zoology and geology, and on January 29, 1839, he and Emma got married. His rooms were too small for the two of them, so they moved into a newer, bigger London house. The first version of *The Voyage of the Beagle* was finally released. Emma became pregnant. Darwin had been elected to a prestigious position in the Geological Society. Everything was as rosy as it could be.

But for reasons no one has ever figured out, Darwin's health took a sudden turn for the worse just when everything started to go right in his life. He had had a few problems on and off ever since 1831, but nothing like this. On any given day he might have an upset stomach, a headache, trembling hands, heart palpitations, insomnia, vomiting, skin rashes, toothaches—even fainting spells. Sometimes they would subside but just as often he'd have several ailments at once.

Some people think he had been bitten by a bug in South America and contracted a rare illness called Chagas' Disease, which can produce some of the symptoms Darwin experienced. Other people think he had inherited poor health from his mother. But many have concluded that his health problems were at least partly psychosomatic—that he unconsciously created the symptoms himself using the power of his mind. People often experience psychosomatic symptoms during times of stress or upheaval. Darwin's life was certainly going through many upheavals in 1839. But medical science was very primitive in those days, and no doctor was ever able to diagnose the problem during his lifetime. Because of this it will probably never be known what was wrong with poor Darwin.

Emma gave birth to their first child, William, in December 1839. Darwin was bursting with pride. He had never thought much about fatherhood,

but he suddenly understood what all the fuss was about. He played with the baby constantly and bragged to everyone how clever little William was. Soon, however, Darwin's inner scientist took over. He started taking notes on what made William cry, what made him laugh, which emotions he seemed born with and which ones he developed as he grew up. Darwin took piles of notes and saved them for years, and much later wrote a book based on his observations of both William and an orangutan at the London Zoo. Darwin had first seen the orangutan in March 1838, and was fascinated with how human this ape looked and acted. He noted that it seemed to have many of the same emotions that humans had. Darwin became convinced that it was too similar to a human child *not* to be related somehow. But this thought was the most forbidden of all.

As Emma raised William, Charles continued writing. Soon enough, his geology book was growing out of control as well, so he once again decided to break it up into smaller books. The first one was going to be about coral reefs. He explained his theory to Lyell, nervous that the geologist would be angry at Darwin for contradicting his own coral theory. Instead, Lyell was so excited by Darwin's idea that he danced around the room. He urged Darwin to write down his theory as quickly as possible. So, for most of 1840 and 1841, except for those days he was feeling sick, Darwin wrote about coral reefs, based on the ideas he developed during his journey. He wanted to make a name for himself as the world's expert on coral. He kept taking notes in his secret transmutation

An orangutan.

notebooks, but for now the "species question" was not his main concern. Meanwhile, Emma had another baby, a girl they named Anne.

The year 1842 was a landmark for the Darwins. He finished and published *The Structure and Distribution of Coral Reefs,* the first book that was truly his alone. Darwin was really an author now. Then he turned his attention back to his secret notebooks, and wrote a 35-page summary of his ideas on evolution. Many people now think of this essay as the first draft of what would later become *The Origin of Species.* To top it all off, Emma was going to have another baby. It was obvious that the family would soon no longer fit in their London home.

The Move to Down House

This turned out to be a blessing in disguise, because both Charles and Emma were tired of London. Dirty, loud, and crowded, with political rallies stomping past their door every other day, it was

Down House.

hardly the place for a serious scientist, his delicate wife, and their small children to live. However, they needed to be close enough to London so that Charles could visit whenever he needed to. They decided to find a place in the countryside and, after much searching, they found their dream house in the village of Down, just 16 miles south of London. The sprawling home, called Down House, was too expensive, but Dr. Robert loaned them enough cash to buy it. They bought it and moved in on September 17, 1842.

This was the last time Darwin would ever move. In fact, it was practically the last time he ever traveled anywhere. Aside from the occasional visits to London, Shrewsbury, and a few health resorts around England, Darwin didn't leave Down House for the rest of his life. The world traveler had come home for good.

Darwin and his family quickly settled into the rambling house and adapted it to their growing family. Their third child tragically died shortly after birth—a common event in those days, as Darwin knew too well from Malthus. But soon Emma became pregnant again. Charles was greatly relieved to have escaped from London. He loved the peace and quiet of the countryside. Concerning his life after moving to Down House, Darwin later wrote in his autobiography,

> Few people can have lived a more retired life than we have done. Besides short visits to the houses of relations, and occasionally to the seaside or elsewhere, we have gone nowhere.... I have therefore nothing to record during the rest of my life, except the publication of my several books.

It was true. From 1842 onward, Darwin's outward life was extremely uneventful. Half the time he was sick and just relaxed at home. When he was feeling well, he'd wake up, take a stroll early in the morning, have breakfast exactly at 7:45, go to his study and write, answer letters from friends between 9:30 and 10:30, write and study until noon, relax a bit in the afternoon, take another stroll, write some more, and then have a quiet evening. Meanwhile, over the years, Emma gave birth to seven more children, for a total of ten.

In his mind, though, Darwin was more active than ever. He collected mountains of facts to support his theories and never once stopped writing or coming up with new ideas for the rest of his life.

Sedentary Scientist

In 1843 Darwin finished the five-volume *The Zoology of the Voyage of H.M.S.* Beagle, with help from a variety of experts on each type of animal. He then turned to writing the next installment of his geology series, about all the volcanoes he had seen, and published it in 1844. Around this time he also struck up a friendship with a young botanist named Joseph Hooker. Like Darwin, Hooker had taken a long natural history expedition as soon as he had graduated from college. His father was director of Kew Gardens, the most prestigious botanical garden in

The Shoulders of Giants

The great physicist Isaac Newton once remarked that he could see so far scientifically because he was "standing on the shoulders of giants." He meant that the achievements of the scientists who came before enabled him to make his discoveries. Science is a cooperative effort; all scientists base their ideas on the advances of those who came earlier. Even Darwin stood on the shoulders of giants. These are some of the people who made Darwin's breakthrough possible.

Empedocles of Agrigento (490–430 B.C.), an ancient Greek philosopher, was the first person to propose the basic idea of natural selection. His notion was that all kinds of strange animals have come into being, but that the strangest animals were one-of-a-kind, and therefore could not find a mate to reproduce. As a result, they all died out. Only those species that were by chance well adapted and could find partners and have babies survived to our time. This concept of passing on useful traits to offspring is fundamental to the modern theory of evolution.

Aristotle (384–322 B.C.), a much more influential ancient philosopher, thought that all the forms of life on Earth could be arranged in a hierarchy: the simplest creatures (such as worms and insects) at the bottom ranging up to the more complex animals (such as mammals and human beings) at the top. This was one of the first attempts to devise a taxonomy of life.

Gregory of Nyssa (331–396 A.D.) and **Saint Augustine** (353–430 A.D.), Christian philosophers, stated that at the Creation, God merely created the laws of nature and the spark of life, and that the world and everything in it slowly evolved according to God's basic principles.

Avicenna (980–1037), an Arab thinker, wrote that "mountains may be due to…upheavals of the crust of the Earth"—the same theory that Lyell and Darwin proved 800 years later.

Galileo Galilei (1564–1642), the famous physicist, showed that scientific theories had to be based on actual observations of the natural world; otherwise, they could not be proved. The ideas of all the earlier thinkers had just been speculation—lucky guesses.

Carolus Linnaeus.

Carolus Linnaeus (Carl von Linné) (1707–1778), in his work *System of Nature,* devised the modern taxonomic system we still use today. He divided all life into two kingdoms, plants and animals, and then divided each kingdom into ever smaller categories: class, order, genus, and finally species. (The further divisions of "phylum" and "family," used by today's biologists, were added later.) Each species was assigned a unique Latin name. He also included human beings in his system, categorizing them as we would any other animal.

Erasmus Darwin

Erasmus Darwin (1731–1802), Charles's own grandfather, wrote that life started as microscopic, primitive creatures in the ocean, which little by little slowly evolved into all the life forms on Earth today. This is exactly what modern evolutionists believe. He also wrote that mankind and apes are closely related biologically. What he didn't know is *why* things evolve.

Jean Baptiste Lamarck.

Jean Baptiste Lamarck (1744–1829) was rightly convinced that species slowly evolved to become other species, primarily due to changes in environment. But he wrongly suggested, as did Erasmus Darwin, that animals grow new features through willpower and then pass these "acquired characteristics" on to their offspring.

Thomas Malthus (1766–1834), in his *Essay on the Principle of Population,* showed that there is a continuous struggle for survival in human society and animal ecosystems, and that only the most successful individuals manage to stay alive long enough to have offspring. This concept was the missing piece that completed Darwin's evolutionary puzzle.

Charles Lyell.

James Hutton (1726–1797) and **Charles Lyell** (1797–1875) demonstrated that the Earth was extremely old, much older than anyone had previously imagined, and that gradual changes had shaped it. An ancient Earth was a necessary part of Darwin's vision of evolution, which required vast stretches of time for species to evolve into each other.

Joseph Hooker.

the country. At the age of 26, Hooker was already regarded as one of the leading experts on plants in all of England. When Darwin asked him to examine his Galapagos plant specimens, they discovered they had many interests in common. He was to become one of Darwin's closest friends.

But 1844 saw the publication of another book that made Darwin extremely upset. Called *Vestiges of the Natural History of Creation,* it was written anonymously. Why? Because it was a book all about the transmutation of species! The author was sure it would cause a scandal. It became the bestselling book of the year. Suddenly, everyone was talking about evolution and species and the origin of mankind. Could it be true, everyone wondered, that mankind was descended from brutish animals? The author had no idea about natural selection and could offer no other believable reason why evolution occurred. Even so, he did make a fairly convincing case that it *did* occur, whether people liked it or not.

At parties all over London people gossiped, "Who is the author?" Many guesses were put forward. One name that kept cropping up: Charles Darwin! *"He's ever so clever, don't you think? Perhaps* he *is the anonymous author."*

Anyone else might have been flattered, but Darwin was furious. The general public loved *Vestiges,* yet most real scientists scoffed at it. The entire book was riddled with errors and misinformation. Darwin wrote to Hooker and asked what he thought of the book. Hooker wrote back, "I have been delighted with *Vestiges,* from the multiplicity of facts he brings together, [even though] he has lots of errors." Darwin, in a very foul mood, replied, "I have also read

the *Vestiges,* but have been somewhat less amused by it than you appear to have been; the writing and the arrangement are certainly admirable, but his geology strikes me as bad and his zoology far worse."

Darwin's old geology tutor, Adam Sedgwick, wrote a cutting review of *Vestiges,* attacking the author for not having the slightest idea what he was talking about. By that time most people had figured out that the real author was a man named Robert Chambers, but Sedgwick's attack (and a letter from Hooker criticizing a different scientist for not really knowing what defined a species) convinced Darwin more than ever that he should not publish his new theory of evolution until he had some more hands-on experience looking at species in detail.

Yet Darwin was also nervous that someone would hit upon the same idea of natural selection and publish it before he did. He was caught in a terrible dilemma. So in 1844 he wrote a more complete version of the theory, a 230-page essay which he hid away where no one could see it. He then gave instructions to Emma that, should he ever die prematurely (he was constantly worried about his health), she should have the essay published as a book. Until then, it would serve as the second draft of the great book he eventually planned to write on the topic.

The Hated Barnacles

By 1846 he was thinking of turning his attention back to "the species question." *The Voyage of the Beagle* had been reissued as a separate book and

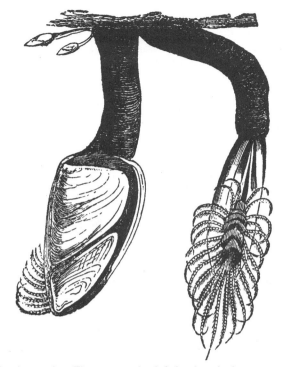

Two barnacles. The one on the left is closed; the one on the right is open for feeding.

was selling well. He had finished all his writing about the zoology and geology of his journey, and after ten years, he was finally *done* examining all his *Beagle* specimens. In a letter to Henslow he wrote, "You cannot think how delighted I feel at having finished." But had he finished? Of all the thousands of specimens he had brought back, boxes and barrels and jars and bottles of insects and mammals and plants and minerals and birds and fish and fossils and much more, there was one—just *one*—bottle left, sitting all by itself in his study. Darwin took it down and looked inside. It

was a barnacle, one of those small, hard-shelled marine creatures that cling to rocks or piers or the undersides of boats. He had found it on a beach in Chile.

Out of curiosity, Darwin peered at it more closely. It was as small as a pinhead—too small even for Darwin's microscope. He got Hooker to send him a new lens, and the strange little barnacle came into focus. How peculiar! Not only was it the smallest barnacle anyone had ever seen, but it lived inside another animal, like a parasite. Darwin thought it would be good practice to describe this new species, so he could call himself an expert when the time came to write his transmutation book. A couple months should be sufficient, he mused, to examine it and write a paper.

Little did Darwin know that one tiny barnacle would consume the next eight years of his life. A perfectionist to the end, he started studying other barnacles to see how they compared. Before he knew it, he was writing a comprehensive study of every barnacle in the entire world, both living and extinct. It wasn't until 1854 that he finished the last of the four books he eventually wrote about his barnacle research. Even his colleagues were astounded that he could spend eight years studying barnacles. Darwin himself admitted in his autobiography, "Nevertheless, I doubt whether the work was worth the consumption of so much time." When he was in the middle of his research and still didn't see any end in sight, he could no longer contain his frustration at the slow pace. "I hate a Barnacle as no man ever did before," he wrote at the time.

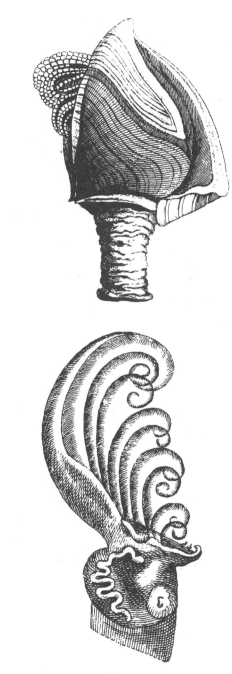

There are hundreds of different barnacle species.

This picture of Darwin was taken when he finished his barnacle research around 1854. People rarely smiled for the camera in those days because they had to sit perfectly still for a long time to get a clear picture.

During those eight years, from 1846 to 1854, the Darwin family had its ups and downs. Charles's father, Dr. Robert, died. Charles and Emma had four more babies, and Down House was filled with children's laughter and games. Charles spent his days hunched over his microscope. His kids grew up thinking that studying barnacles was how fathers spent their time. When they visited friends they would ask, "Where does your daddy do *his* barnacles?"

Charles became sicker and sicker with his mysterious illness. But the one thing that made him sadder than anything else was the tragic death of his eldest daughter, Anne, whom he liked to call Annie. Her illness was as mysterious as his. In 1851 he took her to a health resort called Malvern Spa, but it did no good. She died at age 10, and Charles never really got over it. Every time he saw her picture he burst into tears. He blamed himself, thinking she had inherited her ailment from him. But to this day no one really knows what made Annie sick.

The Road to the Origin

With the hated barnacles finally out of the way, Darwin woke up on the morning of September 9, 1854, with a clear mind and no further distractions from what he knew was the task that would define his career. "Began sorting notes for species theory," he scribbled in his diary that day. This time there was no turning back.

He still had many problems to work out. One, in particular, had been bothering him for years. He could see how organisms could evolve as their environments changed. If, for example, a species of sheep had been living when the Earth passed into one of the Ice Ages, only those sheep with thicker wool would survive the cold winters. Those born with short hair would freeze to death. As the environment got colder, the sheep would evolve thicker coats. But the fossil record revealed that sometimes animals evolved in different directions, even when the environment hardly changed at all. How could this happen? At the end of 1854 the answer came to him. "I can remember the very spot in the road," he wrote, "whilst in my carriage, when to my joy the solution occurred to me."

He realized that, in any ecosystem, there was more than just one "ecological niche," as it is now known. Imagine that a species of monkey migrates into a forest. Two types of fruit grow in this forest: delicious, soft fruits that only grow at the very tops of the slimmest branches of the tallest trees; and tough-skinned fruits that fall to the ground but are hard to tear open and chew. The average monkey is too big and too heavy to reach the fruits on the treetops, and his teeth are not quite strong enough to tear open the fruit on the ground. But because of variation a few of the monkeys are smaller and more agile than average, and they *can* reach the treetop fruits. A few other monkeys are born with stronger-than-average jaws and bigger teeth; they can chew the tough fruits, at least a little bit.

Darwin realized that after a while, the *average* monkeys would eventually starve to death, because they could eat neither the soft treetop fruits nor the tough ones on the ground. But the smaller monkeys would eat the treetop fruits and survive, and have babies that were small like their parents. Eventually, these monkeys would evolve into a smaller, more agile species. Down on the ground, those monkeys with strong jaws and big teeth would eat the tough fruits and survive as well, and have babies with strong jaws and big teeth. And *they* would evolve over time into a different species, different from both the original species of average monkeys and from the smaller species too. The average monkeys—the species that had originally migrated into the forest—would go extinct. Evolution, Darwin saw, can go in two or more different directions at once, even if the ecosystem (in this case, the forest) had not changed at all. This concept, originated by Darwin, is called *the principle of divergence.*

Darwin now felt confident that his theory, when completed, would hold up under the demanding questions of his colleagues. And his reputation was now so good that no one could accuse him of being an amateur.

Throughout 1855, as he prepared to write the final version of his theory, he engaged in more and more experiments to back up his ideas. The first one was to see whether seeds could reach isolated islands by floating across the sea or being accidentally carried by birds. He had mixed results, but showed that it was possible for islands in the middle of any ocean to become populated with plants this way.

He also started breeding pigeons, to show that artificial selection could indeed lead to new types

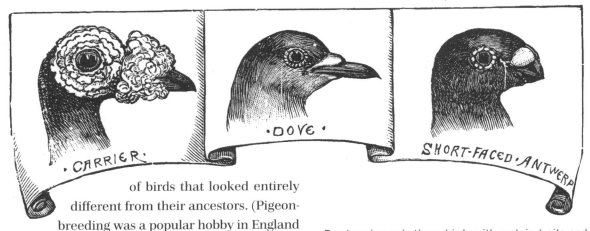

of birds that looked entirely different from their ancestors. (Pigeon-breeding was a popular hobby in England at the time.)

He revealed his theory only to his closest friends, including Hooker and Henslow. They thought it intriguing, but needed to see all the evidence before they were convinced. In 1856, Darwin finally revealed the details to Lyell, who had never really liked the idea of transmutation. But now Lyell liked the theory so much that he begged Darwin to write a paper on the topic as soon as possible, before anyone else could steal his brilliant idea.

Darwin had no excuses now. For the rest of 1856 and 1857, he worked night and day on a "big book" that he planned to call *Natural Selection.* As usual for Darwin, the project quickly started to get out of hand. The more he wrote, the bigger the project got. He'd spend months writing one chapter, only to realize that he needed two more chapters to explain the first. It was becoming like his barnacle research all over again—a neverending project. How long would it take? Four years? Eight? More?

Then on June 18, 1858, Darwin got the shock of his life.

By choosing only those birds with certain traits and mating them for several generations, pigeon-breeders created all sorts of unusual breeds that never occurred naturally.

Traveling Plants

Like many naturalists, Darwin wondered how plants migrated to isolated islands. A plant native to one country might also be discovered growing naturally on an island hundreds or even thousands of miles away, even though it was not brought there by humans. Darwin guessed that some seeds floated across the ocean from one place to the next, either on their own or stuck in pieces of driftwood. Darwin was the first person to do experiments to see if seeds could stay in seawater for a long time and still be able to sprout. He proved that even though most plants cannot survive in a salty environment for long, *some* seeds can float across the ocean and still sprout into plants. This is a smaller version of Darwin's experiment.

What you need

a cup or bowl

salt

various kinds of seeds (good ones to use are peas, cucumber seeds, radish seeds, beans, or asparagus seeds)

several small plant pots, or empty yogurt containers with holes poked in the bottoms

soil

Fill a cup or bowl with water, and sprinkle in enough salt until the water tastes noticeably salty—about one teaspoon (5 ml) per cup (240 ml). Drop two or three of each kind of seed into the water. Some might float; some might sink. Let the seeds soak in the saltwater for two days, as if they were floating in seawater on their way to an island that is a two-day journey away.

After soaking, plant each seed in a separate pot.

Fill your small plant pots (or yogurt containers) most of the way with soil, and pat it down. After the seeds have been in the water for two days, plant one seed in each pot, making sure to create labels showing which kind of seed is in which pot. Push each seed about a quarter inch (6 mm) below the soil level and smooth it over. Place the pots in a sunny location, preferably on a tray or dish. Water the seeds thoroughly at first, and every day sprinkle a little water to keep the soil moist (but not soggy). Wait for the seeds to sprout. It can take anywhere from two days to two weeks, depending of the type of seed; check the seed packets. How many of the seeds sprouted? All? None? Some? Did the salt poison them? It would only take a single seed floating to an island and successfully sprouting to establish that new kind of plant on the island, since the plant would then mature and drop seeds of its own.

5

A Turning Point
in Human Understanding

Surprise Package

For the previous few years Darwin had been communicating with a brilliant young naturalist named Alfred Russel Wallace. Wallace was traveling among the tropical islands of the Dutch East Indies (which is now part of Indonesia), and he sold the rare animal specimens he collected to scientists back in England, including Darwin. The two men had a casual relationship and occasionally discussed ideas during their correspondence. Nothing too serious, just friendly scientific chat.

On June 18, Darwin received his latest package from Wallace. He tore it open without any idea what it contained. Inside was an essay Wallace had written and a note asking Darwin what he thought of it. The essay was entitled "On the Tendency of Varieties to Depart Indefinitely from the Original

Type." As Darwin read it, his eyes widened, his heart sank, and he began to feel faint. Wallace had come up with the exact same theory as Darwin! Transmutation, natural selection, divergence—it was precisely the same, point for point! Not only that, but Wallace's writing was so much clearer than Darwin's. Darwin felt that his entire world had crumbled in an instant. After 20 years of dillydallying, he had been beaten to the punch by a young beginner in some faraway jungle.

Many years later, Wallace would remember how the idea for his essay had come to him while he lay sick in bed in the tropics: "One day something brought to my recollection Malthus's 'Principles of Population,' which I had read about 12 years before. I thought of his clear exposition of 'the positive checks to increase'—disease, accidents, war, famine.... It then occurred to me that these causes or their equivalents are continually

Cartoonists mocked the idea of apes acting human.

acting in the case of animals too.... It occurred to me to ask the question, Why do some die and some live?... It suddenly flashed upon me that this self-acting process would necessarily improve the race, because in every generation the inferior would inevitably be killed off and the superior would remain—that is, the fittest would survive." There was no doubt about it: Wallace had come to exactly the same conclusions that Darwin had. The two men were even both inspired by Malthus. It was also no coincidence that Wallace had read both Lyell's *Principles of Geology* and Darwin's *Voyage of the* Beagle.

As it turns out, Darwin should not have been surprised at all. Wallace had been hinting in earlier letters that he had a big new idea. And Wallace had published an essay three years earlier called "On the Law Which Has Regulated the Introduction of New Species." It contained some speculations about transmutation that seemed similar to Darwin's. Lyell had read it and had immediately told Darwin to read it as well. Transmutation was in the air, Lyell said, and Darwin ought to get his own book published as quickly as possible. But Darwin ignored Lyell's warning and did not seem worried that someone else might publish his idea before he did.

Compromise

Now Darwin looked at his pile of half-finished manuscript pages. What should he do? Had all his work been for nothing? Scientists are always striving to be the first to publish any new idea or theory. Having "priority" meant that you could prove you had invented the theory all by yourself. After reading Wallace's essay, Darwin could no longer claim that he had thought of the idea first. If he were to finish and publish his book now, people might think he had copied the idea from Wallace. Darwin used to think he was above all that; a true gentleman scientist wouldn't concern himself with trivial matters like claiming credit for new ideas. But he found that he *did* care. And it made him feel very ashamed of himself. "It is miserable in me to care at all about priority," he wrote.

That very day he wrote to Lyell, sent him Wallace's essay, and asked in desperation for Lyell's advice.

Lyell consulted with Hooker. They decided on a "gentlemanly" compromise: they would take papers from both Wallace *and* Darwin to a meeting of the Linnean Society, one of the most prestigious scientific organizations in England. Both papers would be published together in the society's magazine. That way, both naturalists would get credit simultaneously. Hooker and Lyell asked Darwin to send them some material about transmutation.

Their timing was terrible. Charles and Emma's youngest child, a baby named Charles Jr., had just died of scarlet fever, and Darwin was too upset to write anything new. So he just sent a copy of a letter he had written a year earlier in which he had described his theory to a famous botanist in America named Asa Gray, as well as a copy of the essay he had written in 1844. That way, at least, everyone

Alfred Russel Wallace, in Singapore.

Alfred Russel Wallace, later in life.

Alfred Russel Wallace

Alfred Russel Wallace will forever be associated with Charles Darwin. This is because both naturalists independently discovered the theory of evolution through natural selection. Yet the two men came from completely different sides of society. Whereas Darwin was wealthy, Wallace grew up poor and remained poor all his life. He was born in 1823 in Usk, Wales (only 80 miles from where Darwin was born in Shrewsbury) among craftsmen and laborers. He went to work supporting himself as a surveyor at the age of 14. He was completely self-educated and never went to high school or college.

Despite these differences in the lives of Wallace and Darwin, there are many amazing similarities in their stories. Like Darwin, Wallace became interested in natural history while hiking in Wales. Like Darwin, he became a beetle collector. Both men read the works of Lyell, Humboldt, and Malthus, and both were highly skeptical about religion.

Just as Darwin had done, Wallace sailed to South America to collect natural specimens. But on the way home from Brazil in 1852, the ship carrying Wallace and four years' worth of scientific specimens sank in the middle of the Atlantic Ocean. Wallace survived for 10 days in a rowboat before being rescued. He lost everything in the disaster and had to start all over again.

Next he traveled to the Malay Archipelago, a tropical wilderness that is now part of Indonesia and Malaysia. He spent eight years there making a living by collecting and selling rare animals to naturalists (such as Darwin) back in England. Wallace too had been pondering the origin of animal species for years, and while in the jungle he wrote several essays on the topic. He knew the one he mailed to Darwin contained important ideas; he just didn't realize how important they were.

When Wallace had begun his voyage to the South Seas in 1854, he was unknown and broke. By the time he returned to England in 1862, he was one of the most famous men in the country, thanks to the controversy over evolution. But he was still broke. Even so, he didn't mind that Darwin got most of the credit for their theory. Wallace felt that Darwin really deserved it more anyway because Darwin had done so much more work presenting all the evidence supporting the case that evolution was true.

Wallace was on to other ideas anyway. He become involved in spiritualism, the belief that living people could speak with the ghosts of dead relatives. Wallace also became convinced that there was life on Mars and that England should be one big commune where everybody shared everything. He never stopped coming up with the most interesting and unusual ideas. But he will always be remembered for just one of them, and to this day he is still honored as one of the fathers of the theory of evolution.

could see that Darwin had come up with the idea first.

Lyell and Hooker read both papers to the Linnean Society on July 1, 1858. Neither Darwin nor Wallace was there—Wallace was still in the Dutch East Indies, and Darwin was too sick and sad to leave home. The meeting took place without them. After the papers were read, "everybody" knew about the theory of transmutation of species through natural selection.

Or did they?

It turns out that only about 30 people were at the meeting. That day there were many other lectures, the meeting went on far too long, and by the end, everyone was bored and just wanted to go home. The papers hardly made any impression at all. In fact, the president of the society later remarked, "The year which has passed has not, indeed, been marked by any of those striking discoveries which at once revolutionize, so to speak, the department of science on which they bear." How wrong he was!

Wallace still knew nothing of what had happened. Darwin was nervous that Wallace might be upset to find out that they had published his essay without his permission and that Darwin himself had claimed co-credit for Wallace's idea. But when Wallace found out, he was actually very pleased. In January 1859, he wrote a letter to Darwin saying he had no hard feelings and was very happy about his essay being published. He was not one of the elite scientists of London, and without the help of Darwin and Lyell his essay might never have been published at all. He was glad to be forever associated with a great man like Darwin. Any other two scientists might have been jealous of each other or gotten into a fight, but for the rest of their lives Wallace and Darwin were friendly and respectful and neither ever said a bad word about the other.

Now or Never

Hooker wrote to Darwin, telling him that now that his theory was known to the public, he *must* quickly write the definitive paper about it before anyone else did. He said the material Darwin gave him for the Linnean Society meeting was too disorganized.

Darwin unhappily agreed to write a short summary of his "big book" on natural selection that was still half-done. Finishing the huge project would take far too long. For now, at least, he would write just an "abstract," a concise outline of the theory. He hoped it wouldn't be longer than 30 pages.

Sorting through his manuscript and a lifetime's worth of notes, he soon realized that 30 pages wouldn't be nearly enough for everything he had to say. Even a summary would have to be much longer than that. As Darwin worked month after month, Hooker told him that, so far, reaction to the published version of the Linnean Society papers had been generally positive. Darwin was relieved. Maybe he had no reason to be nervous. Maybe everyone would like his theory after all.

He wanted to make sure his book was filled with facts that supported his idea. The book *Vestiges of Creation,* which had so upset Darwin, was strongly

Asa Gray.

criticized for being very short on facts. His book had to be more believable. Also, Wallace's essay was really just guesswork. Wallace had hit on the same theory as Darwin, but his essay was far too short to include any facts or evidence to support it. Darwin wanted to make sure *his* book went far beyond what Wallace had written. So he wrote and wrote as fast as he could, touching on every aspect of natural selection, listing as many facts as he could in the shortest possible way.

In May 1859, Darwin was done. But his 30 pages had turned into 500 pages! It would no longer fit into a magazine. It had to be published as a whole book.

John Murray, the same publisher who had released Darwin's *Voyage of the* Beagle, agreed to publish his new book as well. Darwin was concerned that it wouldn't sell many copies and that the publisher would lose money. But Murray assured him that controversial books usually sell well, even if they aren't on popular topics.

Darwin, with a lot of help from Emma and other friends, spent the next few months correcting and proofreading the manuscript. They finished in October and sent the book off to be printed. There was no turning back now. Darwin was exhausted from his year spent writing and was still nervous that people might laugh at his theory. He decided to take a short vacation. He rode up to a health resort at Ilkley in Yorkshire and rested there until his book came out. He was bracing himself in case there was a controversy. He still feared that critics would write negative reviews about the book, or that it would make a few people upset. He had no idea that this one book would create a firestorm of hysteria that would engulf the entire world and forever change humankind's view of the universe.

The Storm Breaks

On the Origin of Species by Means of Natural Selection, or the Preservation of Favoured Races in the Struggle for Life, by Charles Darwin, was published on November 24, 1859. All 1,250 copies were instantly snapped up by eager buyers. The publisher, John Murray, immediately started preparing to print 3,000 more. These might not seem like big sales numbers today, but in 1859 any book that sold that many copies in such a short time was considered a bestseller. Eventually it went into six editions. Darwin was ecstatic. He had expected the book to flop.

Darwin had a bigger concern, however, than tallying sales figures. He wanted to know what everyone thought of his theory. He had done his best in 14 short chapters to lay out his argument, point by point. The first two chapters showed that both domesticated and wild species displayed great variations. Then he presented the principle of natural selection. After that, he tried to explain the theory's weaknesses, such as the absence of transitional forms. Chapter 7 explored the possibility that instincts and behaviors also evolved—not just physical features. He then did his best to unravel the mysteries of inheritance before spending several chapters on geology and the age of the Earth. He finished up by stating that similarities between

Emma Darwin always helped her husband edit and correct his manuscripts. Here she is with their son Leonard.

ON

THE ORIGIN OF SPECIES

BY MEANS OF NATURAL SELECTION,

OR THE

PRESERVATION OF FAVOURED RACES IN THE STRUGGLE
FOR LIFE.

By CHARLES DARWIN, M.A.,

FELLOW OF THE ROYAL, GEOLOGICAL, LINNÆAN, ETC., SOCIETIES;
AUTHOR OF 'JOURNAL OF RESEARCHES DURING H. M. S. BEAGLE'S VOYAGE
ROUND THE WORLD.'

LONDON:
JOHN MURRAY, ALBEMARLE STREET.
1859.

The front page of the first edition of *The Origin of Species.*

species usually show that they are related. He took his readers step by step and tried to honestly discuss every point so that no one could misunderstand what he was trying to say: natural selection works on variations to bring about transmutation of species over long periods of time. He packed the pages with facts and evidence.

Did it make sense to anyone else? Was it ridicu-

lous? One of the first people he asked was his friend Thomas Huxley. The two had met a few years earlier and had quickly grown close. Huxley was a science professor in London and an experienced naturalist. He was very open-minded in his views about evolution. The two friends actually had opposite personalities; while Darwin had grown passive, timid, and hesitant, Huxley was bold, loud, and fearless. He wrote to Darwin as soon as the book came out to say that "no work on Natural History Science I have met with has made so great an impression upon me…. I think you have demonstrated a true cause for the production of species." He didn't stop there; he declared that "I am prepared to go to the stake" to defend *Origin.* In other words, he would risk everything to fend off any critics. Huxley continued, "I trust you will not allow yourself to be in any way disgusted or annoyed by the considerable abuse and misrepresentation which, unless I greatly mistake, is in store for you…. You must recollect that some of your friends, at any rate, are endowed with an amount of combativeness which may stand you in good stead. I am sharpening up my claws and beak in readiness." This was more than Darwin—who was terrified of arguments—had hoped for. Someone to defend his theory in public!

One by one his friends and colleagues wrote letters. Hooker, who had known about the theory for years, of course loved the book. Lyell was full of praise, though he still had some thinking to do about natural selection. Erasmus wrote to say, "I really think it is the most interesting book I ever read."

Thomas Huxley.

Battle Lines

Not everyone was happy about it, however. Adam Sedgwick, who had first taught Darwin to be a geologist, was livid with rage. Sedgwick thought belief in evolution was the road to damnation. Parts of the book he "read with absolute sorrow; because I think them utterly false." More attacks soon arrived. Captain FitzRoy, still a conservative Christian, hated the book and regretted having taken Darwin along with him on the *Beagle*. Darwin would have felt bad enough just reading their letters, but both Sedgwick and FitzRoy wrote newspaper articles attacking the book as well.

Almost immediately the battle lines were drawn. Most of England's freethinking intellectuals hailed *Origin* as a breakthrough in science. But conservative professors, church leaders, and upper-class aristocrats rushed to condemn it. Every time a bad review appeared in one magazine, one of Darwin's supporters would write a glowing review to counter it. Richard Owen, the man who had examined Darwin's South American fossils and one of the most respected scientists in England, wrote a devastating review in April 1860. Darwin was very upset. He had thought that Owen was still his friend. Not any more; *Origin* had a strange way of making everyone take sides. The ideas bursting from its pages were too important to ignore. People either hated it or loved it.

Even so, for the first six months or so, the dispute over *Origin* was confined to the educated classes. But on June 30, 1860, the controversy reached the boiling point. On that day in Oxford was the meeting of the British Association for the Advancement of Science, the most important scientific convention of the year. Rumors starting flying that a major controversy was brewing, and that it was to be settled at the meeting. A thousand people—including many reporters and politicians—showed up to see the fireworks.

Darwin, as expected, was "too sick" to attend. He simply couldn't stand the tension. Huxley, claws sharpened, took his place.

Bishop Sam Wilberforce, a leading cleric considered the most fearsome debater in England, stood up to pass judgment on *Origin*. His speech roused the crowd. He claimed the book was absurd! Blasphemy! An insult to science and religion both! The audience shouted its approval. No one could give a speech like Wilberforce. Before he sat down he turned to Huxley and asked him, "Is it through your grandfather or grandmother that you claim descent from a monkey?" The hall erupted in laughter at the clever insult.

But he had underestimated his opponent. After quickly brushing aside all of Wilberforce's criticisms, Huxley turned to the Bishop and said, "If the question is put to me, would I rather have a miserable ape for a grandfather, or a man highly endowed by nature and possessed of great means and influence and yet who employs those faculties and that influence for the mere purpose of introducing ridicule into a grave scientific discussion—I unhesitatingly affirm my preference for the ape!" He had turned the tables on poor old Wilberforce. The audience screamed in delight.

Going Ape

Victorian Londoners were at first outraged by the suggestion that human beings were related to apes. But visitors who saw the apes at the newly opened London Zoo were forced to admit how human-seeming the animals were.

What you need
pencil
paper

Take a trip to a zoo near where you live. (If there are no zoos in your area, check out or rent a videotape or DVD of a documentary about apes.) Find a place where you have a good view of the chimpanzees, gorillas, or orangutans. Observe them for several minutes (or hours), and try to notice all the ways they look and act human. Take notes and make a list of all the similarities between the apes and people. For example, both ape and human mothers like to cradle their babies in their arms.

Describe not just their physical features but their behavior as well. Now make a separate list describing all the ways apes are *different* from people. For example, the apes are covered in hair, they can't speak in sentences, etc.

When you're done, look at your lists. Which is longer? Are apes very similar to humans, or very different? Do you think we're related to apes?

Descended from the Apes?

The meeting sparked a wildfire. Soon every newspaper and magazine in the country was commenting on the debate and giving its opinions for or against evolution. Darwin had done his best to keep any mention of mankind and apes out of his book but now it was too late. Huxley and Wilberforce put apes on center stage. Were humans really nothing more than glorified monkeys? One aristocratic lady summed up the feelings of Britain's social elite when she declared, "Descended from the apes? My dear, let us hope that it is not true—but if it is, let us hope that it will not become generally known."

No one in England had ever seen a gorilla before.

Cartoonists had fun drawing human-acting animals.

By sheer coincidence an explorer named Paul du Chaillu showed up in London a few months later with news of a new animal he had discovered in Africa—the gorilla! No one in England had ever seen one before. He told tall tales of ferocious gorillas attacking humans, and showed off real gorilla skins he had brought back. Everyone wondered, "Are *these* the apes that we're all descended from?" Darwin's "Ape Theory" was the talk of the town. Magazines ran cartoons of apes dressed in tuxe-

does, of Darwin's head on an ape's body—anything shocking that would stir up emotions and sell more copies.

Darwin hid at Down House, writing dozens of letters every week trying to explain himself to those who would listen. But he couldn't face the public. He left that up to his closest colleagues, Huxley, Lyell, Hooker, and Asa Gray. Together they worked tirelessly to spread "Darwinism" around England and around the globe. Huxley became known as "Darwin's Bulldog" for his tough defense of evolution in any debate.

Despite their loyalty and efforts, in truth Huxley and Lyell never completely agreed with everything in the *Origin of Species*. They still had their own ideas, and didn't follow Darwin blindly. Details needed to be adjusted, points clarified. Darwin's book was merely the starting point; Huxley knew better than anyone that evolution was much bigger than just one man and one book. It was a whole new branch of science.

Darwin was still very sensitive. He was afraid that the arguments over *Origin* would rip society apart. And he listened too much to his critics. As early as the second edition he started making changes in *Origin*. Little by little he weakened his arguments so that people wouldn't be angry at him. By the time the book came out in its sixth edition his reasoning was not nearly as strong. He changed so many words that he began to contradict himself. He should have had more confidence. Experts now agree that the first edition was the best.

Huxley, "Darwin's Bulldog."

Count the Generations

In 1654, an Irish Bishop named James Ussher calculated the age of the Earth by totaling all the generations recorded in the Bible. Ussher's computations were very difficult because many of the patriarchs mentioned in the Old Testament—such as Noah and Methuselah—were said to have lived for hundreds of years and often became fathers when they were already extremely old. Ussher concluded that the world was created on October 23, 4004 B.C.

We now know that he was wrong—more wrong than he could have ever dreamed. The Earth is not 6,000 years old; it's over 4 *billion* years old. And the whole universe is much older than that.

But what if he had been right?

What you need
Pencil
Paper

Let's pretend, for a moment, that Bishop Ussher was correct: the world was created in 4004 B.C. If that's the case, then how many generations of people have been born since then?

Until very recently in history, girls usually got married when they were still young teenagers. Historians say that, on average, a girl would get married at 15 and have her first baby when she was 16. That would mean there were about 16 years between generations.

Take your paper and use it to cover the bottom of this page (so you don't see the answer yet!)

First, calculate the number of years between 4004 B.C. and this current year. Write it down on your paper. How did you come up with your number?

Now you're ready to calculate the answer: If each generation is 16 years from one to the next, then how many generations have been born since 4004 B.C.? Write down your solution. How did you determine this number?

Turn the book upside-down to read the correct solution.

Until Darwin's day, Bishop Ussher's calendar was thought to be true and accurate. His calculations were even included in some editions of the Bible!

Answer: First, add 4,004 to the number of the current year, to get a sum of slightly more than 6,000 years. To find the number of generations, divide the sum by 16; the answer is just over 375 generations.

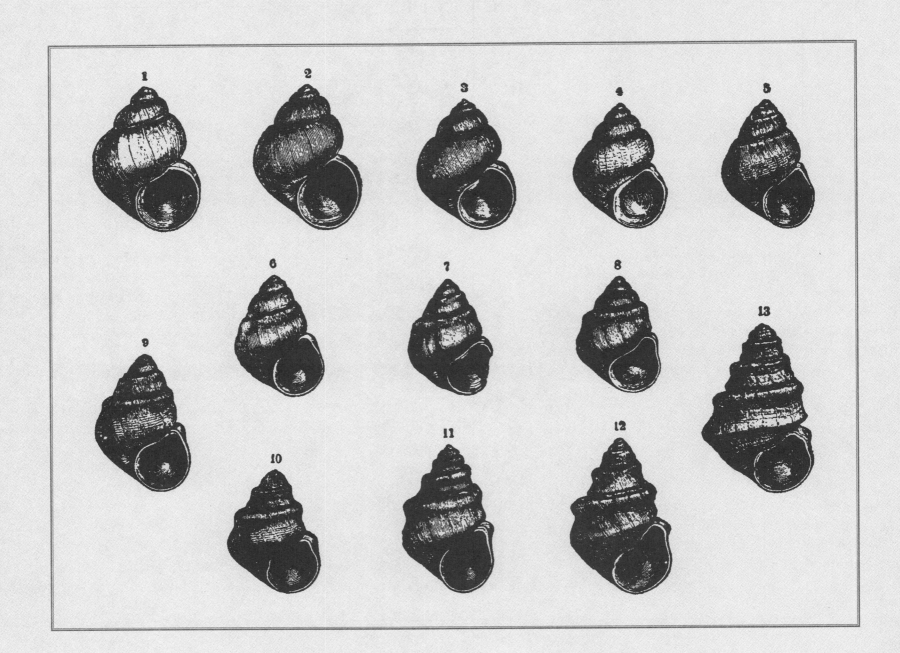

❦ 6 ❧

The Idea That Changed the World

Darwin's Theory of Evolution

Even though the words "Darwin" and "evolution" are familiar to almost everyone, very few people understand how Darwin's theory of evolution actually works. This chapter will explain it in terms that anyone can comprehend. Before you can fully grasp it, however, you'll need to be familiar with the following key concepts.

Variation

No two creatures are exactly the same. If you have brothers and sisters, look at them and compare them to yourself. Are all the children in your family the same height? Do they all have the same shoe size? Same shape of nose? Are some smarter than others? Can some run faster? Are some braver, shier, or nicer than others? The more you look, the more differences you'll find. Yet you and your siblings have the same parents. Doesn't that mean you should all be exactly alike? The answer is no. Every individual person or animal is a unique combination of genes inherited from his or her parents. Like snowflakes, no two individuals can be precisely the same as each other. Even small animals that all look alike—such as mice or goldfish—are, when inspected closely, different from each other in one way or another. These differences between similar creatures are called *variations*.

The biological reasons for variation were not discovered until the 20th century, long after Darwin's lifetime. But, like Darwin, we don't need to be experts in genetics to know that variation occurs all the time. It's easy enough to observe variations with your own two eyes.

All creatures exhibit variations. These fossilized seashells are all from the same species, but each shell is unique.

Heritability

Did you ever notice that children tend to look like their parents? No one is ever an exact copy of his or her mother or father, but parents and kids are always somewhat similar. Does your mother have two arms, two legs, two eyes, a head, ten fingers, a mouth, and a brain? Then you do as well. If your parents have big noses, odds are you'll have a big nose too. If your parents have brown skin, you will have brown skin. If your parents are short, you'll probably be short. This is true in every family.

And it's not just true in human families. A Siamese cat will always give birth to Siamese kittens—it will never give birth to a puppy, an alligator, or even a different breed of cat. This may seem obvious, but it's an important aspect of evolution. Even the smallest features can be passed on from parent to offspring. The word for this is *heritability*. As with variation, the exact biological cause for heritability was not discovered until after Darwin had died. Even so, farmers, animal breeders, and parents all over the world know that heritability is one of the basic features of all species.

Overpopulation

In the natural world, all animals and plants produce many more offspring than can ever survive. For example, think about a pair of adult rabbits. The average female rabbit gives birth to a litter of four baby rabbits, five times a year. (Many types of rabbits can have more offspring than this per year; this is just an average.) After one year, that first pair of rabbits will have made 20 baby rabbits (4 babies × 5 times a year). Half of these (10) will be female rabbits. Each of these 10 young female rabbits will grow up; after about six months they can start having babies of their own. After another year, all of the 10 female rabbits will themselves each have given birth to 20 more rabbits—10 females and 10 males. Now you'll have at least 200 rabbits (10 mothers × 20 babies). The next year those 100 female rabbits will produce 1,000 more females. Then 10,000, then 100,000, and so on. After only 12 years you'll have over a trillion rabbits! Soon enough, the entire world would be completely covered in rabbits.

Now imagine this: the same tendency to overpopulate is true for almost every species. Frogs and goats and bees and fish and pigeons and a million other kinds of animals. The name for this tendency of organisms to produce more offspring than they need is *superfecundity*. If every baby animal survived, there would be uncountable numbers of every kind of animal filling every square inch of the planet, with millions more appearing every day, without end.

But this obviously isn't the case. So, where do they all go?

The Age of the Earth

In Darwin's time, no one really knew how old the Earth was. Some people thought it was only 6,000 years old. Others thought perhaps 30,000 years, or 100,000. But discoveries in geology and paleontology throughout the 19th century indicated that the planet was much older than that—millions of years

Make Your Own Geological Strata

Early geologists proved that the Earth was at least many millions of years old by inspecting geological strata visible in exposed cliffs. This proof of the planet's age was an important factor in the acceptance of the theory of evolution, because animals need a long time to evolve. It's not always easy to find a place near your home where real strata are visible, but you can make your own strata with materials you find in your backyard and kitchen.

What you need
a tall glass jar with a lid, preferably with the label removed
several plastic or paper cups
Choose five to eight of the following:
dark soil
light soil
sand
crushed dry leaves
dark gravel
light gravel

small pebbles
dry or crushed cement powder
plaster of paris powder
salt
flour
small macaroni or crushed noodles
instant coffee
sugar
dried beans or lentils
hot chocolate powder
unpopped popcorn
crushed cereal

Put each ingredient into a separate cup, and divide the cups into two categories, light and dark. (Put the flour, the light soil, the popcorn, and the sand on one side, for example, and all the dark ingredients on the other side.) Make sure the jar's label has been removed (and the glue that was attaching the label as well), and that it is dry. The taller the jar, the more strata will be visible.

One by one, gently pour about a quarter-cup of each ingredient into the jar, alternating between light and dark. Do not tilt or shake the jar while you are filling it up. Make each layer between half an

inch (12 mm) and an inch (25 mm) thick. If the top of the layer is irregular when you first pour it in, gently tap the side of the jar or smooth down the top with a finger or spoon. The layers need not be perfectly even. Try to use each ingredient at least once before starting over with a second layer of the first ingredient. Remember to alternate light, dark, light, dark.

When you are almost finished, fill up the jar to the very top with the last layer, so there is no empty space in the jar at all. Tightly screw on the jar lid. Now you have your own personal jar of strata. Inspect the different layers and imagine them full of fossils, crystals, and mysteries from the Earth's past.

If there were fossils in your strata, where would the oldest fossils be found? Why? If a paleontologist compared fossils found on two different layers, what would the paleontologist be able to say about the fossil found on the lower layer?

old, at least. Darwin knew that evolution took a long time to happen, so he was very concerned with proving that the Earth had been around for a long time.

He need not have worried. It was not until the 20th century that scientists were first able to accurately measure the Earth's age, using very sophisticated techniques. We now know that the Earth is about 4.5 *billion* years old! That's hundreds of times older than anyone in Darwin's era even imagined. And it's more than enough time for evolution.

Changing Environments

In most cities and states the weather is usually the same from one year to the next. In Phoenix, it is very hot every summer. In Minnesota, it snows every winter. Weather patterns pretty much stay the same. At least they seem to during the space of a single lifetime.

Over long periods of time, however, the Earth's climate and environment have gone through many, many changes. Long ago, the Sahara Desert used to be covered with plants. Hawaii wasn't even an island—it was under water. During the Ice Ages, much of Europe and North America were buried in ice. Throughout the Earth's history, its climate has shifted back and forth many times in many different ways. It's even happening right now; the whole planet is getting warmer and warmer every year. Meteorologists predict that in a hundred years, the weather around the United States (and elsewhere) will be quite different than it is today.

Darwin knew that changing environments were an important element in his theory. Every time an environment shifts, the organisms in that environment must adapt to survive.

Evolution Through Natural Selection: Darwin's Theory Explained

Darwin spent years thinking about variation, heritability, overpopulation, the age of the Earth, and changing environments. He was trying to understand the origin of animal species. One day, the final piece of the puzzle clicked into place.

This was his brilliant insight: Every type of animal produces far more offspring than can survive. Most baby animals die before growing up. If not, the world would long ago have become overrun with animals. How do they die? Some are eaten by predators. Others starve to death. Others die of disease. Some grow to adulthood but can't find a mate and never have any offspring. Only a few actually succeed in growing up and reproducing.

But why do some die and others survive? What's so special about the survivors? Are they just the lucky ones? The answer, Darwin realized, lay in the variation among members of the species. Not all animals in any species are exactly the same. Those animals with some features that helped them avoid predators, get food, or find mates more successfully tended to survive longer than their brothers and sisters who lacked those features. Only the animals best adapted to their environment would survive long enough to grow up. Those animals that were weak or slow or foolish would tend to be the first ones to die. Darwin called this *natural selection,* but people often like to call it *survival of the fittest.*

The few surviving animals would reach maturity and have offspring. Because of heritability, their offspring would tend to resemble the well-adapted parents. Since the parents were generally the ones with the most useful features, they would pass those features on to their offspring. This way, all the harmful variations would die out, but the useful variations would be passed down and spread. Darwin's term for this was *descent with modification.*

But what if the animals' environment changed? The features that helped survival wouldn't necessarily remain the same. As generations passed, animals with new and different variations would be the ones surviving and passing their traits on to their children. The more the environment changed, the more the species would have to change to survive in it.

Darwin realized that with enough time, an animal species could accumulate so many changes that it would no longer resemble the original species from which it descended. He called this process *transmutation through natural selection.* All that was needed to turn one species into another was time—countless generations of animals changing little by little as they adapted to their shifting environments. And his own investigations had shown him that the Earth was indeed old enough for evolution to explain the existence of every single living thing. Darwin felt that all people, all animals, and even all plants were related to each other. At some point in the distant past a microscopic living organism first appeared, and all life forms on Earth were descended from that one tiny creature.

So here's Darwin's theory of evolution in a nutshell:

1. Any group or population of organisms contains variations; not all members of the group are identical.
2. Variations are passed along from parents to offspring through heredity.
3. The natural overabundance of offspring leads to a constant struggle for survival in any population.
4. Individual organisms with variations that help them survive and reproduce tend to live longer and have more offspring than organisms with less useful features.
5. The offspring of the survivors inherit the useful variations, and the same process happens with every new generation until the variations become common features.
6. As environments change, the organisms within the environments will adapt and change to the new living conditions.
7. Over long periods of time, each species of organism can accumulate so many changes that it becomes a new species, similar to but distinctly different from the original species.
8. All species on earth have arisen this way, and are thus all related.

Certain animals, such as this lemur, are well adapted to climbing trees. Even so, lemurs seem closely related to humans because their body shape is so similar to ours.

Evolution in Action: The Peppered Moth

People used to think that the transmutation of species took such a long time that it could never be directly observed. But sometimes we can actually see natural selection happen in nature over the span of just a few years. Darwin did not know it at the time, but an example of rapid evolution was happening in England during his lifetime. He would have been overjoyed if he had been able to observe it himself.

In northern England lives a type of insect called the peppered moth, whose wings are speckled with white and black spots. These moths prefer to rest on trees that have light-colored bark and whitish lichen growing on them. The local birds love the taste of these moths and eat them whenever they can. But the moths' wings serve as camouflage; the speckled white-and-black coloration blends in with the bark and lichen, making them hard to notice.

At the beginning of the 19th century most of these moths had lighter-colored wings with more white speckles than dark speckles. A small percentage liked to rest on darker trees and so had darker wings. But as the Industrial Revolution progressed, the factories of northern England spewed so much coal smoke into the air that the pollution not only killed the lichen but also covered the trees in soot. The moths' environment changed. Now, when the lighter-winged moths landed on the darkened trees, the birds could easily see and eat them. Only the darker-winged moths remained camouflaged. They avoided being eaten by the birds and survived to have offspring that inherited their darker wings. Little by little, the number of moths with darker wings started to grow. Naturalists carefully studied peppered moths for years, and by 1900 they counted that 98 percent of the moths had dark-speckled wings! Most of the light-winged moths had been eaten and had not reproduced more of their kind. Transmutation through natural selection had been directly observed just a few miles from where Darwin was born.

The story of the moths is not over. Starting in the 1950s, England passed strong new air-pollution laws that limited the amount of exhaust coming from factories. By the 1990s most of the pollution had been eliminated. As a result, lichen grew back on the trees and the light-colored bark was again visible. Now the situation was reversed. The dark moths were plainly visible against the light background, and the birds ate them. But the few remaining light moths blended into the background, and they survived. Accordingly, the moths have evolved back to the way they were before—now most of them are light-colored again!

Air pollution in 19th-century England was much worse than it is today.

Is That Everything I Need to Know About Evolution?

There's more to evolution than what's been discussed so far; biologists happily spend their whole lives studying it. Often, the more people learn about evolution, the more questions they have. To get you started, here are answers to some of the most common questions about evolutionary theory.

Does evolution really make animals change shape? Can I see it happen?

That would be exciting, but unfortunately the answer is no. Evolution is not like a science-fiction film with special effects showing an alien creature growing a new head. Given enough time, evolution can make a *species* change shape, but not an individual animal. Every plant, animal, and person remains the same throughout its whole life. *Groups* evolve, not individuals. You'll never be able to see a fish grow legs and start to walk; evolution doesn't work that way. What evolution does is control what percentage of a group's individuals possess a certain trait or feature.

Does evolution always *happen to every species? Or do some animals never change?*

You might think from the description of evolution that natural selection is always working to bring about changes in species. But in reality most of the time natural selection *prevents* evolution from happening. Most of the variations and new features that might arise in organisms are not helpful at all, because evolution has already been going on for a very long time. Every species has already adapted to its environment as best as it can. Just about any change to a species would end up hurting it. Natural selection is continuously "weeding out" those variations that make an organism less adapted to its environment. Natural selection usually leads to evolutionary changes only if a species' environment and living conditions are shifting. In many cases, animals and plants that live in a stable environment hardly evolve at all. Horseshoe crabs are a famous example. They're fairly common on beaches around the world today. But archaeologists have found fossils of horseshoe crabs that look exactly like modern horseshoe crabs—except that the fossils are over 200 million years old. Horseshoe crabs have not evolved one bit in all that time because their environment—shorelines and beaches—hasn't changed much either.

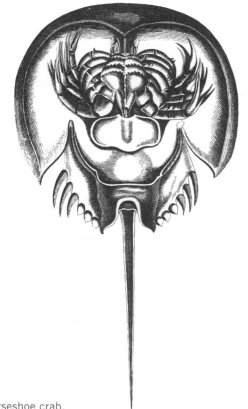

Horseshoe crab.

Is evolution the same thing as "progress"?

Not necessarily. During the Industrial Revolution and the Victorian era, people thought that history was always progressing forward, that life got better and more advanced every day. So they naturally assumed that evolution worked the same way. It seemed that life on Earth had started as a tiny organism and had *progressed upward* through evolutionary changes to become the complex and superior creatures known as human beings. Yet Darwin showed that evolution does not always imply advancing toward more complicated or larger forms. Many animal species a hundred thousand years ago were larger than they are today; changes in climate made them evolve *downward* to become smaller. Other species, such as the peppered moth, evolve *sideways* (by changing color) but do not become any more or less advanced. Species merely adapt to their current environments. But that doesn't mean they're getting "better."

Are animals and plants really "perfect" in their design?

William Paley's Divine Watchmaker argument relied on a basic assumption that all animals were "perfect," intentionally designed like a watch to have all the right parts in all the right places. But Darwin and other naturalists discovered this was far from true. Animals often have weaknesses and deficiencies that could easily have been improved upon or eliminated if someone had designed them from scratch. Many animals have *vestigial organs,* body parts that don't work and for which the animal has no use. Various kinds of snakes, for example, have leg bones. Why would God give snakes leg bones if they have no legs? Evolutionists will tell you that snakes evolved from earlier reptiles that *did* have legs—legs which slowly disappeared as the species changed. The *external* legs disappeared, that is; the useless leg bones continued to exist inside the snakes' bodies. And if every species was "perfect," then why don't all animals have the best possible features: flawless vision and hearing, strong and fast legs, big brains, sharp teeth, and so on? Most don't, because each species is just a hodgepodge of adaptations. Animals aren't "designed" to be any way at all; they're just an accumulation of evolutionary changes, some of which no longer serve any purpose.

What is a "hopeful monster"?

Darwin was careful to point out that evolution does not happen in sudden jumps from one generation to the next, but rather in small steps. It's extremely unlikely, for example, that some long-ago horse just happened to be born with black-and-white stripes, and that all modern zebras are descended from this one freakish striped horse. These freaks of nature were later called *hopeful monsters.* (Deformed and freakish animals *are* born every now

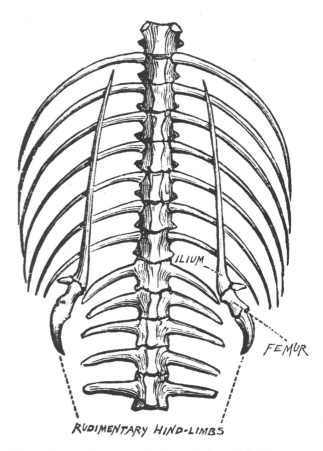

This python skeleton reveals the snake's vestigial leg bones, which serve no function.

and then, but their deformities almost always hurt rather than help their chances for survival.) Many people in Darwin's era mistakenly thought that evolution required these "hopeful monsters" to work, an idea which was ridiculed as being impossible. As a result, Darwin worked hard to show that evolutionary changes happen very gradually, and that his theory did not depend on the existence of freaks.

Natural Selection: A Closer View

Natural selection happens in many different ways. Animals have evolved countless strategies to find food, avoid being eaten by predators, attract mates, and survive all kinds of dangerous situations. Any trait that allows an animal to survive and reproduce is "chosen" by natural selection because the animals with that trait will pass it on to their offspring. These are just some of the fascinating adaptations that various animals have developed through natural selection.

Camouflage

Camouflage—markings that help an animal blend into the background—is one of the most common adaptations in nature. It's the easiest way to avoid being seen by predators. (Remember the peppered moth?) Green tree frogs are barely noticed when they're sitting on green leaves. Some animals change their colors according to the seasonal changes in their habitat. Jackrabbits are brown in the summer, making them hard to see against brown leaves and soil; in winter, their fur changes to pure white so that they're camouflaged against the snow. Chameleons don't have to wait for a new season. These lizards can change their skin color in seconds to match any color of their surroundings.

Predators also use camouflage, to keep a low profile while hunting. The golden brown color of a lion's fur is the same color of the dry grass where it hides while stalking prey. A bright pink lion would have a lot of trouble sneaking up on its victims!

Mimicry

Some animals use *mimicry*—imitating or pretending to be something else—to help them survive. Certain butterflies and moths have spots on their wings that look like scary eyes; from a distance

The wings of the Eyed Hawkmoth mimic the eyes of a much larger animal. The moth uses them scare off predators.

STICK INSECT.

The "walking stick" is an example of both mimicry and camouflage. The insect so closely resembles a real stick that it cannot be recognized by its enemies.

Camouflage Egg Hunt

In the natural world, predators are always looking for something to eat. The easiest way to escape them is to blend into the background so they don't notice you. Animals that are *camouflaged* have the same color and patterns as the environment around them. A predator will generally notice, catch, and eat only the most easily captured prey; after its belly is full, there is no need to keep hunting. This activity will demonstrate how the principle of camouflage can help organisms survive.

What you need
1 dozen eggs
stove and pot
a set of colored felt pens, or crayons
a friend (or relative)
pencil and paper

Ask an adult to hard boil a dozen eggs for you. Once the eggs have boiled for seven or eight minutes, cool them down by running cold water over them in the sink or placing them in the refrigerator.

Put all 12 eggs back in the carton and bring them, along with a friend, outside to a natural area with grass, dirt, bushes, and other plants. Your backyard or front yard is the best place for this activity, but a park is fine too. Bring a set of colored felt pens—make sure to have a selection of greens and browns—or crayons (pens work better on eggs) and a pencil and paper.

Sit down in a comfortable spot. Look at the surrounding environment and choose pens that match the colors of the plants and other features around you. You and your friend should then take three eggs each and, one by one, draw camouflage designs on them. Use different colored pens to match the shadows and stripes and other patterns you see. Think about where you might be placing these eggs when deciding how to camouflage them. If you are going to place them in the grass, use a variety of greens. If you are going to place them in a bed of dried leaves, use browns and grays. Remember to leave six eggs plain white, completely uncamouflaged.

Once you're done coloring, ask your friend to close his or her eyes while you place all 12 eggs around the yard or park. For the experiment to work properly, the white and colored eggs should be placed in similar locations—you shouldn't hide all the camouflaged eggs in the most difficult spots while leaving the uncamouflaged eggs out in the open. For every white egg you place in the grass, place a camouflaged egg in the grass. After the eggs have been hidden, ask your friend to look around and pick up the *first* six eggs he or she finds. After six, have your friend stop looking and bring all six back to you.

On one half of your paper write "Camouflaged," and on the other half write "Uncamouflaged." Make a mark under each heading for each egg found.

If the color of an egg's shell didn't make any difference to your friend, the "predator," he or she should find, on average, just as many camouflaged eggs as white eggs: three of each. But how many of each kind did your friend *actually* find?

Retrieve the remaining six eggs, then repeat the experiment, but this time have your friend hide the eggs while you close your eyes and then search. Write down the data from the new trial. Repeat the experiment several more times until you begin to see a pattern in the totals.

Did the coloring on the eggs help or hurt their chances of being detected by a predator?

they look like the eyes of a large predator, so birds are afraid to eat these butterflies. The "walking stick" is an insect that looks so much like a twig that you can scarcely tell it apart from the real thing, even up close.

Speed

This one's obvious: the faster an animal can run, the better it can escape from whatever's chasing it. Most animals have evolved to run as fast as they possibly can, considering their size, body shape, and environment. Predators have to go fast too, or they'll never catch their prey. A cheetah chasing a gazelle is a sight to behold!

Deception

Animals that are slow and easy to catch sometimes develop ways of tricking their enemies into going away. Opossums and certain kinds of snakes will occasionally pretend to be dead, hoping that whatever is fighting them will lose interest and leave them alone.

Deterrence

One way to avoid being eaten is to be hard to eat. Armadillos have tough, bony plates covering their bodies; when they curl up into a ball, there's no way for a predator like a wolf to get inside. Porcupines and hedgehogs are protected by hundreds of dangerous, sharp spines.

Toxicity

If something's poisonous (toxic) or tastes bad, then predators will quickly learn that it's not good to eat. This strategy is most common among plants, insects, and fish.

Acute Perception

This too is one of the most common adaptations in nature. The better any animal can hear, see, or smell, the better it can hunt for prey or detect predators before they get too close. Some animals have developed all kinds of amazing perception systems that we humans don't have. Dolphins and bats use sonar (bouncing ultrasonic waves off prey) to hunt. Scorpions and elephants can detect vibrations in the ground. Owls and ocelots have acute

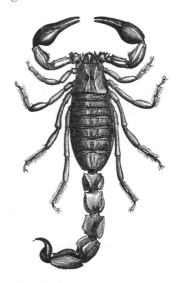

Scorpions can "hear" vibrations in the ground with special sensors on their legs.

Where Are the Missing Links?

Ever since Darwin's day, critics of evolution have pointed out the absence of what have become known as "missing links." (Scientists prefer to call them "transitional forms.") If, as the zoologists claim, bats evolved from mouselike rodents, then where are the fossils of the creatures that were halfway in-between—a mouse with partial bat wings? None has ever been found. If there's no evidence of transitional forms between two species, then how can we be so sure that evolution really happened?

Here are *five* good answers to that question.

1. **Missing links *do* exist.** Difficult as it may be to visualize, all modern birds are the descendants of prehistoric dinosaurs. Scientists have uncovered several fossils of the missing link between dinosaurs and birds, a transitional form called Archaeopteryx that looked like a flying lizard with feathers. They've also found many bones and fossils of transitional forms between ancient primates and modern apes and humans, both of which are descended from the same ancestors. Many other transitional forms in the evolution of horses and reptiles have also been found.

The Archaeopteryx was an animal halfway between dinosaur and bird. This drawing, based on actual fossils, shows what it might have looked like.

2. **At least 99.99 percent of all the fossils in the world have not yet been discovered.** They're not easy to find! But paleontologists are searching for them every day, all over the world. So we haven't found all the missing links...*yet.*

3. **Only in the rarest of circumstances do animal remains become fossilized to begin with.** True, scientists have not found the fossils of most transitional forms, but neither have they found the fossils of most "stable forms" either. The fossils may never have been created in the first place. Unless the conditions are just right for creating fossils, animal remains and bones will quickly disintegrate and disappear. Since transitional

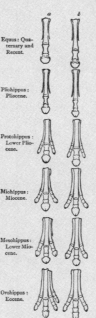

Various transitional forms in the development of the horse. The earliest fossils, at the bottom, show that horses once had toes. By modern times, at the top, the horses' middle toes had evolved into hooves, while the other toes gradually disappeared.

forms probably occurred under changing environmental conditions, it's unlikely that their skeletons would be preserved undisturbed for millions of years.

4. **Evolution does not happen at a consistent rate all the time.** Most plants and animals will remain in the same environment for extremely long periods—millions of years, in some cases. As long as their environment stays the same, the animals won't evolve very much, if at all. But when organisms are forced into a new environment, they must adapt quickly to survive. In a relatively short span of time (perhaps as little as 100,000 or even 10,000 years, which is like the blink of an eye in geological terms) a species could radically evolve, passing through many transitional forms. When it reaches a

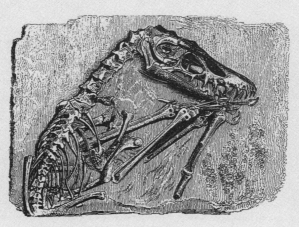

Most dinosaurs, such as the one preserved in this fossil, evolved only slightly over millions of years because their environment was stable. When the environment suddenly changed, many of them went extinct, and the rest evolved very rapidly into other forms.

form that is best adapted to its new environment, that species will remain stable and essentially stop evolving for a long time again. This stop-and-start aspect of evolution is called *punctuated equilibrium,* because stable, perfectly balanced ecosystems (equilibrium) are occasionally interrupted (punctuated) by rapid change. As a result, almost all fossils are laid down during times when species aren't changing, which is why transitional forms are rarely found.

5. **Many top scientists answer the question in a completely different way: every fossil ever found is a transitional form!** *All* organisms, living or dead, are transitional forms from one species to another. It just depends on how you look at it. The animals of today could be considered transitional forms between their ancient ancestors and

the unknown creatures into which their descendants will evolve far in the future. Maybe human beings will one day be thought of as the missing link!

night vision and can see in almost total darkness. Even dogs can hear sounds that humans can't hear.

Dietary Diversity

Animals have acquired all kinds of adaptations that allow them to eat a wide variety of foods. Giraffes, of course, have evolved long necks to reach leaves on the tops of tall trees. Cows have four stomachs that allow them to eat and digest grass, which most animals cannot digest. Some animals have developed an immunity to poison, which allows them to eat other animals that have evolved to be toxic!

Even plants have evolved unique strategies for getting food. Venus flytraps catch insects in their leaves and dissolve them with special digestive fluids. A sundew snares bugs on its sticky hairs; the plant then swallows up its prey and digests it. Darwin was so fascinated by these carnivorous plants that he spent years researching them.

Choosing Partners

If camouflage is so important for survival, then why are some animals brightly colored? How can natural selection explain something as flamboyant, beautiful, and seemingly useless as a peacock's tail? Peacocks with smaller, duller tails would be less visible to predators, so it seems that they would be more likely to survive and that colorful tails should never have evolved. Yet they have. Why?

The answer is a form of natural selection called *sexual selection*. While it is not as important as other aspects of natural selection, it does account for many of the features that otherwise seem to have no evolutionary explanation.

Darwin's theory of sexual selection states that an animal must do more than merely stay alive to pass its traits on to later generations—it must also have offspring. And the only way to have offspring is to mate with a partner. So evolution will tend to favor those animals that are best at attracting mates. Unattractive animals will tend to have fewer offspring, and their features will die out.

But what determines "attractive"? This is a mystery no one has yet figured out. Whatever the reason, we do know that many animals regard certain features as especially appealing. Peahens (female peacocks) think that the peacocks with the flashiest tails are especially handsome. As a result, the most colorful peacocks have the most success finding partners, have the most offspring, and pass on the flashy-tail genes to the next generation. Over the years, the peacock species thus evolved to have colorful feathers. Dull peacocks may have had more success avoiding predators, but they left fewer offspring.

The same principle holds true with many other animals and features. The females of some bird species show a preference for male birds that do a mating dance. Male frigate birds and hummingbirds flap and fly and chirp in amazing displays that can last for hours. Sexual selection has preserved these seemingly strange behaviors.

Other behaviors related to sexual selection are not about impressing the females: they're about in-

A peacock using its tail to attract a mate.

timidating rival males. Bull elephant seals become extremely aggressive and violent around mating season. The bossiest males get more partners not because the females like them any better but because they've scared away all the other males.

More than Just an Idea

It's not hard to imagine why it took Darwin twenty years to write the *Origin of Species,* his book about evolution. The basic idea was clear to him, but there were so many details to work out, so many questions that had to be answered. In fact, he never felt that he had properly explained his theory. To Darwin, *Origin* was just a brief *summary* of the arguments for evolution. Before events forced him to describe his theory as quickly as possible, he had been planning to write a book about evolution that was 10 times as long!

He also wanted to make sure his idea stood up to any possible criticism. He spent years accumulating evidence and facts to back up his theory. Often, he made the investigations and confirmed the facts himself. It was essential that his theory was *scientifically rigorous,* or confirmed by scientific observations. This was a new way of doing things in natural history. The earlier evolutionary thinkers were just that—only thinkers. Their theories had just been speculations. No one really knew whether or not their guesses were correct. Darwin, on the other hand, wanted to make sure that evolution was the only possible explanation

for all the factual evidence he had collected from geology, anatomy, paleontology, and biology.

Those aren't the only reasons Darwin was reluctant to go public with his theory. He knew from the beginning how controversial his idea would be. Few people had ever before dared to imply that humans were related to apes. But he hated controversy. He never argued with anyone, and the thought of speaking in public frightened him. Like any proper Victorian gentleman, he wanted to avoid scandal at all costs.

Yet he was a scientist, with a duty to reveal the truth as he knew it. He was caught in a terrible dilemma. In the end, he felt he had no choice; he published his theory, no matter what. It was a brave thing to do.

Sure enough, the response to *Origin* was immediate and explosive. Speakers insulted him. Preachers condemned him in their sermons. All of society was scandalized. "How dare this man question the unique and lofty status of the human race," they demanded. "Is he suggesting that we are descended from monkeys? How dare he say we were not created in God's image! This book is an insult to the Bible," they said.

Fearing just these kinds of attacks, Darwin purposely never mentioned in the *Origin of Species* that human beings were the result of evolution as well. But it didn't matter. Everyone jumped to that conclusion. Philosophers began to ask questions that Darwin could not answer. If, as everyone agrees, each human being has a soul, then when did we as a species acquire our souls? As far as anyone knew, animals didn't have souls, but if evolution is

The Benefits of Beauty

According to the theory of sexual selection, being attractive is sometimes more important than being strong or clever. Birds with big flashy tails attract more mates—but they also can attract more predators. Is it really worthwhile to have an attractive feature if it only makes you more likely to be eaten? This activity shows how visually striking traits can become common in a species even if they seem to hurt chances for survival.

What you need

8 nickels (or any other small, plain objects, such as buttons, erasers, macaroni noodles, checkers, etc.)

40 pennies (or any other small, pretty objects, such as marbles, candies, plastic toys, hair ornaments, etc.)

This activity is a simple version of a life-simulation game that scientists use to model how evolution works. The game will show how certain features can spread throughout a population over several generations.

In this game, the objects all represent male members of the same species—a plain-looking kind of bird we'll call the Dum-Dum Bird. The nickels are the standard form of the species—bland and unremarkable, having evolved to avoid predators by blending into the background. But a new variation in the Dum-Dum Bird population has arisen—a few of the males now have some bright red feathers. This new variation is represented by the pennies.

The female Dum-Dum Birds are attracted to the males with red feathers. But the color also draws the attention of the foxes—predators that like to eat Dum-Dum Birds whenever they can.

The rules:

At the start, 80 percent of the birds are plain (nickels), and 20 percent have red feathers (pennies). With each passing generation, only one-fourth of the plain birds get eaten by foxes; but *half* of the red birds get eaten. On the other hand, each plain bird will be lucky to find one partner willing ever to accept him, so he will leave just one male offspring over his entire lifespan. The red birds, however, are so popular with the female birds that each will leave on average 4 male offspring over his entire lifespan. In both cases, the offspring will inherit the same coloration of their fathers.

How to play:

Place 10 coins (or other objects) in a row: 8 nickels and 2 pennies. This is your first generation of 80 percent plain birds and 20 percent red birds. Now, apply the rules described above to this generation (and all later generations). One-fourth of the plain birds will be eaten by foxes, so remove one-fourth of the nickels: 2 nickels. Half of the red birds will be eaten, so remove half of the pennies: 1 penny. You're left with 6 plain birds and 1 red bird.

Now it's time to make the next generation. Each plain bird will leave only one plain male descendant, so slide all 6 nickels down a few inches. But each red bird will leave 4 red male offspring, so place 4 pennies adjacent to the nickels in the new row.

You're now on the second generation. Notice how the population has changed: even though a greater percentage of red birds was eaten before they could leave offspring, their mating success has paid off. In the second generation the plain birds are down to 60 percent of the population, and the red birds are up to 40 percent.

Repeat the process for 3 more generations. Round all numbers up: one-fourth of 6 will be 1.5, which you should round up to 2. What happens to the population of Dum-Dum Birds? At the end of the game, what percentage of the birds will be plain (nickels), and what percentage will have red feathers (pennies)?

This is how sexual selection works: species can evolve to acquire appealing but harmful adaptations, because reproductive success is just as important as survival. Beauty has its benefits!

1st Generation

2nd Generation

3rd Generation

Answer: Second generation: 6 nickels and 4 pennies
Third generation: 4 nickels and 8 pennies
Fourth generation: 3 nickels and 16 pennies
Fifth generation: 2 nickels and 32 pennies

true then long ago we were animals just like any other. Was there some moment in history when an intelligent monkey first acquired a soul and became a human being?

Darwin did not realize it at the time, but he changed forever the way the human race sees itself and the world. And he changed how scientists search for the truth.

7

Reluctant Celebrity

Sundews and Orchids

In the summer of 1860, while the evolution debate was raging, Charles Darwin took his family on vacation. His daughter Henrietta was sick, so the whole family visited relatives in a town not far from Down House. While Henrietta was recovering, Darwin went walking in the countryside to clear his mind. One day he happened to notice a strange little plant that had trapped an insect in its hair-covered leaves. As he bent down to watch, the plant slowly curled around the unfortunate bug. Darwin had read about these plants before and knew they were called *sundews,* but he never really gave them much thought. Sundews were carnivorous, meaning they survived by eating meat. This was extremely unusual among plants; most survive simply on sunlight, water, and minerals from the soil. Darwin was suddenly fascinated.

How did these unusual plants become carnivorous? In what other ways were they different from ordinary plants? And could it be possible that these weren't even plants at all, but rather a strange kind of animal with roots and flowers?

He dug up the sundew and brought it back to the house. He planted it in a pot and started performing experiments. He dropped bits of meat on its sticky hairs. He watched as they slowly curled inward and digested the meat with special fluids over a period of days.

Darwin was hooked again. After exhausting himself beyond measure with his writings on transmutation, he had felt he could never be interested in anything again. Yet throughout his life he would be seized by all-consuming passions for various topics. Modern psychologists now think that Darwin had what is called an *obsessive personality,* an uncontrollable habit of becoming fascinated

Did God merely create the spark of life and the laws of nature, letting evolution take its course? Or did God create each species individually?

109

Carnivorous Plants

Y ou too can grow your own carnivorous plant. Venus flytraps are native to the United States, so they're fairly easy to buy. Call your local plant stores or nurseries to see which ones carry them. If Venus flytraps aren't available in your area, you can always buy them on the Internet. You can find a list of online sites that sell carnivorous plants at http://www.sarracenia.com/faq/faq6280.html.

What you need
one or more Venus flytrap plants

Follow the instructions that came with your Venus flytrap on how to care for it and keep it thriving. They are delicate plants and require special attention. In many areas of the country the atmosphere is too dry for flytraps to grow outside or even in a pot. If you live in a dry area, you'll have to grow them in an enclosed container, like a terrarium. And remember to always keep the soil moist! Flytraps are native to swampy areas that are always damp.

If no insects naturally land in the traps, you will have to feed your plant yourself. It's fascinating to watch the leaves close around a victim, as long as you don't have too much sympathy for the bug. If you experiment by trying to feed your flytrap food that is *not* alive, it will "spit out" the food by opening its trap leaves before they fully close. The reopening process can take up to 12 hours. And don't stimulate the flytrap's "trigger hairs" too often. After several false alarms, an individual pair of leaves will lose the ability to close ever again.

Darwin tormented his carnivorous plants with all kinds of inedible meals, but there's no need to repeat his experiments at the expense of your vegetable pets.

To complete your investigations, check out a video of the film *Little Shop of Horrors,* a funny fantasy about a carnivorous plant that eats humans. It's good for a laugh, but don't worry. Venus flytraps can't even hurt your finger, much less eat you alive.

with something while ignoring everything else.

His obsession with carnivorous plants lasted for years. But he soon added yet another obsession: orchids. These beautiful flowers grew naturally near Down House, and during his walks, Darwin became fascinated by their unusual relationship with insects. As with the sundews, he brought some home and started investigating them in detail. He realized that the orchids relied on specific insects for pollination. A bee or fly or moth would be attracted a flower of a certain shape, stick its head into the flower to eat the nectar, accidentally pick up some pollen, and then deposit it in the next flower. In this way the orchids all fertilized

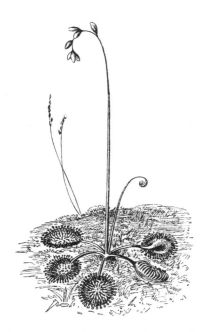

A sundew. A leaf on the right has captured an insect in its hairs and has curled inward to digest it.

each other and made seeds for the next generation. Each type of orchid was unique and attracted only certain insects, and could only be pollinated in a certain way. Darwin saw that this was a prime example of *co-adaptation,* in which two or more different species evolve together as a group. Both the orchids and the insects needed each other for survival.

Soon Darwin asked Hooker to send him rare orchids and carnivorous plants from Kew Gardens, the leading botanical garden in England, where Hooker worked as a director. Darwin wrote letters to other botanists all around the world and acquired a huge collection of exotic orchids and carnivorous plants. He was once again consumed with new passions. Or was he just trying to withdraw from the controversy his book had started?

The Idea That Wouldn't Die

Meanwhile, it was up to Huxley to lead the charge for evolution in London. Huxley coined the word *Darwinism* to describe Darwin's specific vision of natural selection. To this day, people still call themselves *Darwinists.* His name has become part of the language.

Huxley gave lectures and wrote articles boldly declaring that human beings had descended from ancestors who were apes. He went out of his way to stir up emotions. Half of London thought the idea was scandalous; the other half thought it was jolly fun.

Joseph Hooker helped Darwin with his researches by sending him exotic plants from all over the globe.

In 1862 and 1863 three important new books were published: Darwin's *On the Various Contrivances by Which British and Foreign Orchids Are Fertilized by Insects,* Huxley's *Man's Place in Nature,* and Lyell's *Antiquity of Man.* All three supported the notion of transmutation of species through natural selection. Darwin's orchid book showed that the flowers must have evolved specifically to attract insects. Huxley presented all the evidence that mankind was the product of evolution as well. And Lyell described new archaeological finds of ancient humans that lived tens of thousands of years ago, long before the supposed date of the biblical creation. Little by little, the case for evolution was getting stronger. But Darwin was still too fearful and awkward to convince people in person. As always, he continued to work behind the scenes, piling up evidence day after day, year after year.

The year 1863 was important for another reason. An amazing new fossil had been found in Germany and brought to London. Richard Owen, the anatomy and fossil expert, examined the specimen and dubbed it Archaeopteryx, meaning ancient (*archaeo*-) wing (-*pteryx*). It was extremely old and appeared to be half lizard and half bird. It had the teeth and tailbones of a lizard and the feathers and wings of a bird. Anatomists had already suspected that birds originally evolved from reptiles, due to the similarities of the body structures of the two different classes of animals. Could Archaeopteryx be the missing link between reptiles and birds, proving once and for all that evolution really occurred? Many scientists thought so, and even today Archaeopteryx is considered one of the clearest examples of a transitional form. Poor Owen, who was violently opposed to evolution, ended up producing some of the best evidence in its favor!

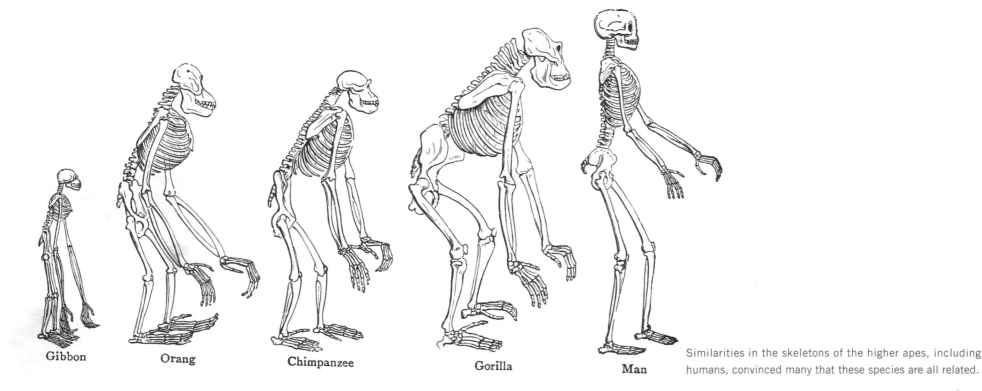

Gibbon   Orang   Chimpanzee   Gorilla   Man

Similarities in the skeletons of the higher apes, including humans, convinced many that these species are all related.

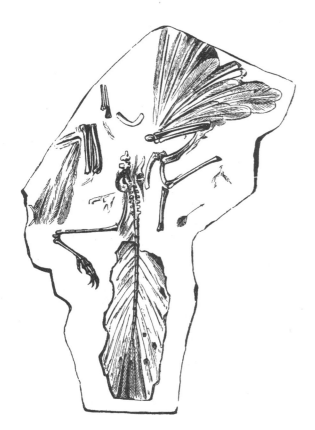

This fossil of *Archaeopteryx* proved to be the missing link in the evolution of birds.

Sickroom Celebrity

In September 1863, while he was reading *Antiquity of Man,* Darwin's health suddenly failed. His usual symptoms flared up—throwing up, skin rashes, exhaustion—but this time they were much worse than ever. He went to a health resort where the experts suggested he take freezing baths every day. The treatment only made him feel worse, and by the time he came home he was sicker than he had ever been in his entire life. His doctors had no idea how to cure him.

Darwin canceled all meetings, appointments, and responsibilities. For the next four years he stayed home and saw almost no one. He rested in bed or in a chair most of the time and only worked two or three hours a day at most, writing letters or tending to his plants. He stopped shaving and grew a big beard that turned white. He became weak and frail. He quickly changed into an old man. Later, when he finally went out to meet people again, even his closest friends didn't recognize him.

All the time that he hid away in his sickroom, Darwin was becoming one of the most famous people in the world. His books were translated into French, German, Russian, and many other languages. His ideas on evolution began to spread far beyond the close-knit world of British natural scientists. Linguists, economists, psychologists, philosophers, anthropologists, and experts from many other disciplines began to see how evolution applied to their work too. Darwin was hailed as the hero of this new way of thinking.

Darwin grew a beard in the 1860s. This is how he is remembered now, but for most of his life he didn't have a beard.

A Theory That Touched Everyone

In 1864 Huxley formed the X Club, a group of nine leading scientists. It was similar to the Lunar Society that Charles's grandfather Erasmus Darwin had joined a century earlier. The club met to discuss evolution and related topics, and to plan strategies for promoting Darwin's ideas in public.

Seed Strategies

A few of Darwin's books—like the *Origin of Species*—were filled with wide-ranging ideas on grand topics. But most of his books, like the ones he wrote about barnacles and orchids, focused on very specific topics. Any book that examines in detail one carefully defined single theme is called a *monograph* (from the Greek *mono-,* meaning "one," and *-graph,* meaning "writing"; thus a monograph is "writing about only one thing"). In this activity, you will write a monograph about a topic of great interest to botanists: seed distribution.

What you need
a notebook
a blank book or several lined pages of writing
    paper stapled together.

In a monograph, the goal is to keep the focus as narrow as possible: instead of writing about seeds in general, you will write only about how individual seeds are distributed from their parent plant to where they will eventually sprout.

Before you write your monograph, collect data by investigating seeds in your environment. Use the skills you learned in the *Be a Backyard Naturalist* activity (see page 17). Collect as many different kinds of seeds and seed containers as possible, such as dandelion seeds, burrs, foxtails, berries, maple seeds, acorns, and pinecones.

First, write about the evolutionary advantage of plants that can spread their seeds far and wide, as opposed to other plants whose seeds drop straight to the ground. Next, inspect each kind of seed and describe in detail the amazing techniques it uses to get as far away from the parent plant as possible. Here are some of the seed strategies you might discuss:

- Dandelion seeds, which look like little parachutes, can float away.
- Burrs are covered in tiny hooks that snag on animal fur.
- Berries are sweet and tempting to birds, which swallow them and pass them on through droppings.
- Acorns are round and heavy and can roll down slopes.
- Maple seeds spin around like tiny helicopters and fly on the wind.

Describe any other strategies that you think the seeds might use. If you want help with ideas, research seed distribution in a library or on the Internet. Keep writing until you feel you've covered every aspect of seed distribution, and you've said everything there is to say. If you want your monograph to be truly scientific, write down the titles of all the books and Web sites you used for research in a *bibliography* at the end of your notebook.

Writing a monograph is a good way to become an expert on any topic.

Because all its members had important positions in the government, universities, and magazines, the X Club became very influential. Huxley would stop at nothing to get evolution accepted as the official view of the scientific community.

In April 1865, while sick in bed, Darwin received some sad news. Robert FitzRoy, the former captain of the *Beagle,* had killed himself. Darwin remembered how moody and miserable FitzRoy had often felt on the ship. Things had only gotten worse as FitzRoy grew older. Even though he had been promoted to admiral and had become famous for setting up meteorological (weather forecasting) stations all around the country, FitzRoy would still get upset at the smallest setback or insult. As a conservative Christian, he also felt guilty that he had unwittingly helped Darwin gather information for his theory of evolution, which he felt now undermined the Bible. FitzRoy never forgave himself. In the end he just couldn't stand it anymore. Despite their differences, Darwin mourned for his old friend.

Around this time an influential sociologist named Herbert Spencer coined a new phrase: *survival of the fittest.* Spencer was a strong supporter of Darwin, but he took the whole concept of evolution further. Spencer declared that *everything* is the result of evolution, not just animals and plants. Social structures, economic systems, and just about anything else evolved, he wrote. Spencer felt that the term "survival of the fittest" was more general than "natural selection," so he used his own phrase in his writings.

His ideas became so popular, and he was such a strong supporter of Darwin, that people began to use "survival of the fittest" even when describing Darwin's theory. Many people told Darwin that Spencer's phrase was more direct and memorable than "natural selection," which was harder to picture and grasp. So, a bit reluctantly, Darwin revised later editions of the *Origin of Species* to include the notion of survival of the fittest. As a result, most people now think it was Darwin's idea in the first place. (There is more about Herbert Spencer's influence in Chapter 8.)

Ahead of His Time

Even though he was often too sick to work, Darwin put every ounce of his strength into researching and writing books that supported his theory. After years of effort, in 1868 he finally released a book called *The Variation of Animals and Plants Under Domestication.* All his years spent breeding pigeons and growing plants in his greenhouse had paid off. As its title suggests, the book was about how domesticated animals and plants have individual differences, and how those traits are passed from one generation to the next. Animal breeders had made use of these variations to intentionally create new breeds. From any group of pigeons, for example, they would choose and mate the male and female with the biggest tails, and repeat the process with the next generations, until they produced a new breed of pigeon with gigantic tails. Darwin's goal was to show that the same process happens in nature, but without mankind's intervention; nature itself would do the "selecting."

On that issue Darwin more than successfully proved his point. But he tried to go one step beyond. He attempted to figure out where variations come from and why they occur. Unfortunately, he was too far ahead of his time. He was trying to write a book about genetics before anyone even knew what genetics was. Chromosomes, DNA, genes—none of these had been discovered yet. No one had the slightest idea how traits were passed from parents to offspring. Darwin did his best to explain it with theories of his own, but they weren't very convincing. He described how microscopic "gemmules" in every cell of the body contain information on how to duplicate themselves. His imagined "gemmules" were in fact somewhat similar to the DNA molecules that were discovered almost a century later. But without powerful microscopes and complex laboratory experiments, Darwin could not know the true nature of his "gemmules." That would have to be discovered by later scientists.

Though few people knew it then, in a small town in central Europe a quiet Austrian monk named Gregor Mendel was already unlocking the secrets of genetics even before Darwin had written his book on variations. Mendel's careful experiments on pea plants, demonstrating the laws of heredity, were published in a German-language journal, but almost no one read it. Darwin never learned of Mendel's experiments, which is a tragic misfortune for science. (There's more about Mendel in Chapter 8.)

The Descent of Man

By 1868, thanks to the popular press, international translations of *Origin,* and the endless efforts of Huxley and the X Club, evolution was no longer a taboo subject. Any book about humans evolving from apelike ancestors was sure to be a bestseller. Dozens of eager authors wrote evolution books of their own. Surprisingly, most of these books made Darwin feel worse. Few of the authors seemed to truly understand his theory, and several of them tried hard to prove him wrong. Darwin wished that someone would write a book about human origins that wasn't full of errors and misconceptions. But who? He realized that if he wanted to read such a book, he'd have to write it himself. When he first wrote the *Origin of Species,* he had been too afraid to mention the evolution of mankind, fearful of causing a scandal. But by the end of the 1860s the idea had become so common that he didn't have to worry about that anymore.

For over two years he sifted through his notes, collected the opinions of experts, and wrote nearly every day. In 1871 his most daring book, *The Descent of Man, and Selection in Relation to Sex,* was published. Darwin's main thrust was to bring together, in one place, all the best scientific evidence that humans—like all other species—had evolved from earlier forms that are now extinct.

As usual, Darwin didn't merely give a few facts or examples here and there. Instead, he built a mountain of evidence from every imaginable field, all of which suggested that mankind had evolved

Darwin built this greenhouse at home, in which he grew tropical plants and performed many botanical experiments.

Theology vs. Science: Room for Both?

Is there really a conflict between the notions of evolution and Divine Creation? Many people feel perfectly comfortable accepting them both. The first person to do this was the Reverend Charles Kingsley, a famous religious writer who told Darwin that "it is just as noble a conception of the Deity to believe that He created a few original forms capable of self-development into other and needful forms, as to believe that He required a fresh act of creation to supply the voids caused by the action of His laws." In other words, "Isn't it miraculous that God had the foresight and ability to create one original lifeform that could evolve into millions of others?" To Kingsley (and many Christians today) this seems even more wonderful and miraculous than the idea of God being compelled to create each species one by one. Darwin was so pleased by Kingsley's view that he included a quote from the reverend in the second edition of *Origin.*

Those who insist that every word in the Bible is literally true are upset by Darwin's ideas. Yet the theory of evolution contradicts only one short passage in the Bible. What about the thousands of other parts of the Bible that are either illogical, in conflict with science, or not historically true? (One famous example: if Adam and Eve were the first humans, and Cain and Abel were their only early children, then how could Cain have had a wife, as it says in Genesis? There are hundreds of similar questions about the Bible.) For anyone trying to prove that every word in the Bible is literally true, evolution is just one of many problems.

Darwin never intended to cause a division between science and religion. He was merely trying to describe nature as he saw it. Many people now think it's possible to be religious and accept scientific truths at the same time. They believe that God created the first life, God created all the amazing laws of nature (*including* evolution), and everything on Earth came from these two creations. To accept evolution does not mean one also has to abandon one's religious feelings.

from primitive ancestors. Here are just some of the points Darwin used to bolster his case.

Comparative Anatomy

Humans, apes, and other mammals share many features in common. Some of these shared features are obvious. For example, there are only minor differences between the basic skeletons of humans and apes, and even their brains are quite similar. Moreover, many features that look different on the surface are in fact closely related. The hand of a man, the paw of a dog, the flipper of a porpoise, and even the wing of a bat all have the same bones in the exact same order; they've just evolved to be longer or shorter depending on whether they're used for grasping, walking, swimming, or flying. Darwin concluded that the only explanation for all these similarities was that all the species were related.

Evolutionary Remnants

If humans are not evolved from earlier species, then why does the human body possess so many *evolutionary remnants*—features and structures that have no apparent purpose? At the base of everyone's spine is a bone called a coccyx—what most people call a tailbone. Why do we have tailbones if we don't have tails? It would make no sense for a creator to give us a bone with no function. But it would make plenty of sense, Darwin argued, if our ancestors once had tails that slowly evolved to be shorter and shorter until all we had left was one

small bone. Similarly, most animals have muscles that let them move their ears back and forth for better hearing. Humans normally can't move their ears anymore, but everyone still has ear-moving muscles, even if you can't see or feel them. Only a few lucky people are able to use them. We also have organs called appendixes, but they too seem to be *vestigial organs,* evolutionary leftovers from

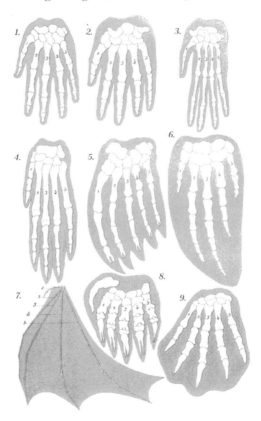

This diagram shows how all mammals have the same bones, but in different proportions. 1. Human hand. 2. Gorilla hand. 3. Orangutan hand. 4. Dog paw. 5. Seal flipper. 6. Porpoise flipper. 7. Bat wing. 8. Mole paw. 9. Duck-bill platypus paw.

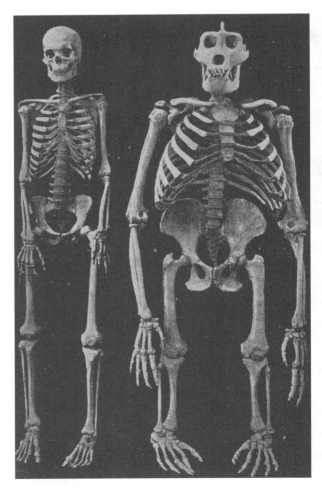

Skeletons of a man and a gorilla. How similar are they?

a time in our species' development when they had a function we no longer need. How else can these features be explained except through evolution?

Embryology

An embryo is an unborn animal during the early stages of its development, when it is still not much more than a tiny cluster of cells in its mother's womb. In Darwin's time, anatomists had recently discovered that the embryos of humans and other animals look almost exactly alike during the first weeks of development. Only after an embryo has grown into a fetus (an older, larger, and more mature embryo) is it possible to tell what kind of animal it will become. Darwin saw this as the clearest evidence that all animals have the same basic biological origins, and that they are all related.

Mental Capabilities

People in Darwin's era thought the main difference between humans and animals was that humans had minds capable of emotions, language, and

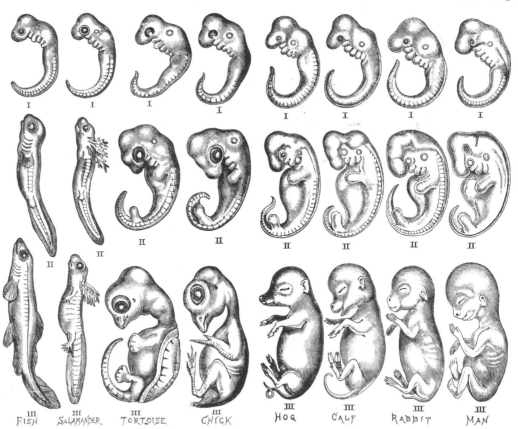

III FISH   III SALAMANDER   III TORTOISE   III CHICK   III HOG   III CALF   III RABBIT   III MAN

The top row shows the embryos of various animals at an early stage of development. They are almost all identical. By the middle row they are slightly older and start to look different. On the bottom row they have matured much further and it is possible for the first time to see which animals they will become.

other types of advanced thought. People believed that animals did not have these same mental abilities. Darwin presented evidence that animals *do* have feelings, that they communicate in primitive "languages" (birds' singing, cows' mooing, etc.), and that they even occasionally use tools. He showed that the difference between the minds of animals and humans was not nearly as great as people supposed. The existence of the human brain was not proof that we are separate from other species.

The second half of Darwin's book was about sexual selection, which is similar to natural selection but is based on how animals choose their mates. As discussed in Chapter 6, animals of all types—insects, reptiles, birds, and mammals—have developed features and behaviors whose sole purpose is to attract mates. Because the most "attractive" organisms mated most often and created the most offspring, *their* features were passed on more frequently and became widespread. Darwin believed that sexual selection explained why the males and females of various species looked different from each other. Decorative or appealing features, such as the tails of certain male birds, evolved to impress members of the opposite sex. It also explained, he wrote, why people from different parts of the world look different from each other. Skin color, hair texture, facial shape—all these were merely the result of men and women in different parts of the world preferring one kind of beauty over another.

Once again, Darwin was ahead of his time. He was trying to give a scientific basis for human evolution, but none of the famous "missing link" fossils from Africa had yet been found. Darwin did not have access to the strongest evidence for his thesis. Not until a hundred years later did paleontologists find actual fossils showing once and for all that humans evolved from apelike ancestors millions of years ago.

If *The Descent of Man* had been published in 1859 (as *Origin* had been), it would have caused a huge outcry. But by 1871 few people were shocked at the idea of apelike ancestors. So, although *Descent* sold quite well, it didn't cause much of a splash. Darwin finally stated quite plainly that humans and apes were related, but it didn't really change many people's minds. By 1871 you either accepted evolution or you rejected it. More evidence wasn't going to sway anyone. The book was most popular with cartoonists, who filled magazine pages with more caricatures of Darwin as a monkey. In any case, Darwin was glad to have finally finished the book.

Half a Wing

Darwin's satisfaction about his new book was spoiled by a fresh attack on his theory of evolution. It was published just as *Descent* was being released. Darwin regarded the attack, written by a biologist named St. George Mivart, as the most serious threat to his whole scheme so far.

Mivart made an interesting point. If natural selection leads to the development of new features, what purpose would a half-formed feature ever

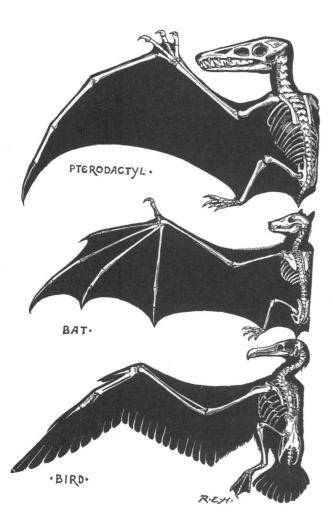

How could these wings have slowly evolved if half a wing serves no function?

serve for the animal that possessed it? If some long-ago rodent was the ancestor of modern bats, Mivart reasoned, then at some stage there had to be a creature halfway in between: a rodent with rudimentary wings that were not yet strong enough to enable the creature to fly. But if it could not yet fly, then the wings only got in the way and did no good at all. As a result, through natural selection, those creatures would die off, as they were not well-adapted to survival. Thus it seems that natural selection would *prevent* the evolution of any new anatomical features. In short, Mivart asked, "What good is half a wing?" Darwin's theory must be incorrect, Mivart claimed.

Darwin was upset because the question was a difficult one, and because Mivart was such a talented writer. Could it be possible that Mivart was right? Would Darwin's theory of natural selection come crashing down and be soon forgotten as a passing fad? Darwin struggled to find an answer to Mivart's challenge. He tried to patch up his theory in the sixth and final edition of the *Origin of Species,* but in some parts he only muddled things even further and didn't completely refute Mivart's challenge.

Scientists have since given two separate convincing answers to the "half a wing" problem. Firstly, there *are* many animals, past and present, that essentially *do* have half a wing. Flying squirrels are a type of rodent with a winglike membrane that stretches between their front legs and back legs. They can't actually fly with these semi-wings, but they can glide, like paper airplanes, from branch to branch. Certain kinds of tree snakes can

make their bodies go flat and also glide, as if on wings, among the trees. Flying fish, lizards, and frogs can all glide through the air with "half-wings" made of fins, skin, or feet. So it seems plain enough that Mivart was wrong—plenty of animals *do* find half a wing useful. Maybe they can't quite fly with it yet, but gliding or being able to fall gently to the ground is also a useful skill that would be passed on through natural selection. The same principle also holds true with other organs, such as the eye. Being able to see a little bit is better than being completely sightless. Every improvement helps, so an eye could have evolved step-by-step as well.

The second answer is more subtle. Many complex anatomical features may have originally evolved to serve an entirely different purpose from what we might think. Primitive lungs in ancient fish species were not used for breathing; they were used for buoyancy, to help the fish float up or down in the water. After a long time the primitive lungs evolved the ability to absorb oxygen, eventually enabling the fish to breathe above water and evolve into amphibians. Feathers and wings probably first evolved *not* for flying but to regulate body temperature, helping dinosaurian proto-birds cool down (by spreading their wings) or keep warm (by ruffling their feathers) as needed. Only later did they use feathers and wings for flying. *Prehensile* (grasping) tails probably first enabled baby mammals to cling to their mothers' fur; later, the tails slowly began to be used for swinging on trees. So, in answer to Mivart, no creature ever really did evolve a useless half-lung, half-wing, or half-tail. These emerging features were always useful for some purpose, even if the features are used for different purposes now.

Emotions

But Darwin had little time to wrestle with all these problems. He was too busy putting the finishing touches on his next book, *The Expression of the Emotions in Man and Animals,* published in 1872. Ever since the 1840s, when he watched the orangutan at the zoo and also took notes on what made his baby son William laugh and cry, Darwin had been fascinated by the emotions of children and animals. He touched on the topic in his *Descent of Man,* but this new book went into the concept in more detail. Darwin felt that if he could show that humans and animals had the same feelings and used the same facial muscles to express those feelings, then he could show that humankind was related to the animals, thus bolstering his case for evolution. People still generally believed that humankind's unique ability to feel and express grief, joy, pride, and jealousy were what made us different from the "lower beasts." Darwin was out to prove everyone wrong.

The Expression of the Emotions in Man and Animals turned out to be one of Darwin's most popular books ever, not necessarily because people agreed with his theories, but because it had pictures! Few books had pictures in those days, and Darwin made sure that he had plenty of funny and unique photographs to illustrate his points. People snapped up copies, and Darwin earned more money from this book than from any of his others.

Darwin showed that animals have emotions just as humans do. This drawing from his book illustrated a cat feeling afraid.

The Last Years

Despite his growing fame as one of Europe's greatest scientists, Darwin spent his later years comfortably at home with his family. He never cared much about being a celebrity. All he cared about was making scientific observations and drawing interesting new conclusions from them. In his twi-

Emotions Left and Right

Darwin was fascinated by facial expressions and was one of the first people to examine them scientifically. Other researchers have continued investigating where Darwin left off. A recent study found that people express their emotions more intensely on the left sides of their faces than they do on the right sides. This experiment will help you see if that is really true.

What you need
10 or 20 photographs of family and friends
a blank index card or piece of white paper
sheet of paper
pen or pencil

Darwin used many photographs, including this one of a young girl, to illustrate how people expressed their emotions. Which side of her face is happier?

Have your parents help you find 10 or 20 photographs that show people's faces close up. Candid snapshots are the best. Try to look for photographs in which people display a variety of emotions: happiness (smiling, laughing), sadness (crying, frowning), anger (scowling), boredom, and so forth.

Spread the photographs out in front of you.

Choose one to start. Take a blank index card or small piece of white paper and lay it so that its edge runs right down the center of the person's face in the picture. At first cover up the right side of the picture. (Be very careful to remember this detail:

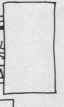

because the person in the picture is facing you, the *left* side of his or her face is on the *right* side of the picture.) Look at the visible half of the face and evaluate how much emotion it shows. Then carefully slide the card over and cover up the left side of the photograph, so that you now the see *other* half of the face. Examine the person's expression again. Does it seem more happy, less happy, or about the same? More or less sad, bored, or excited?

On a separate sheet of paper, make three columns. Label the first column "Left Side of Picture (Right Side of Face) More Intense." Label the second column "About the Same." Label the last column "Right Side of Picture (Left Side of Face) More Intense." After you've decided which half-face in the first picture is more intense, make a mark in the appropriate column. Set the picture aside and choose another one. Repeat the observation process with each picture, making a note in the appropriate column every time.

When you're done, add up the columns. Which side wins? Is it really true that people express their emotions more intensely on the left sides of their faces?

light years, he continued to work without interruption and published an amazing series of specialty science books, mostly about plants. Even though none of these books was nearly as important or groundbreaking as *Origin* or *Descent,* they all sold well because he was so famous.

He and his devoted wife Emma still watched over Down House as their children grew up, moved out, and got married. Darwin was by now a stately old man. Though he was only 62 when *Descent* was published, his illness had made him look much older. He had a daily routine: he'd wake up, take a walk, write a little, putter around in his garden and greenhouse making botanical observations, read and answer letters, scan the newspapers for any mention of his books, write a little more, and rest. It was just what he needed—a slow pace with few interruptions. Because of the relaxed atmosphere, his health during his last years was actually better than it had been for decades.

Darwin's study, where he did all of his writing.

Darwin's home at Down House, shown as it looked after he had lived there a long time.

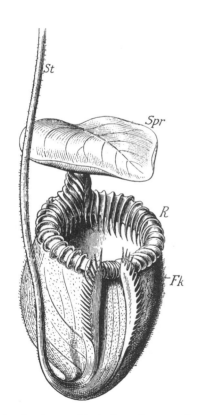

St

Spr

R

Fk

Darwin wrote about every kind of carnivorous plant, including this pitcher plant (also known as *Nepenthes*), which traps insects in its bowl.

Darwin never thought of himself as a genius or as anyone particularly important. He was annoyed when people showed up at his house uninvited, just to get a glimpse of the great man. Someone once sent him a questionnaire asking if he had any "special talents," to which Darwin replied, "None." Universities and clubs began awarding him honorary degrees; he accepted them in good humor.

After years of observation, he finally finished his book *Insectivorous Plants* in the summer of 1875. What had started as a fascination with sundews had grown to include all plants that eat insects. He was the first person to write a book about these organisms, which are among the strangest in the world. Darwin tried to understand how plants—which did not even have nervous systems, much less brains—could detect their prey and know what to eat. He never could figure it out, but the book was a fascinating overview of the subject in any case. He followed it up shortly afterward with a small book on a related topic: plants that use tendrils to help themselves climb up fences and walls.

In 1876, Darwin was persuaded to write an autobiography, because his many fans were curious about his life and career. He wasn't comfortable writing about himself, so he wrote it very quickly, and as a result it ended up as a haphazard collection of memories. He barely mentioned his life-changing journey of exploration, saying he had already written about it in *The Voyage of the* Beagle. As to the other parts of his life, he just pieced together a snippet here or a little story there, never saying a harsh word about anyone. He almost never revealed his inner feelings.

He couldn't stand being away from his research for long. Over the next few years he published three more books, all of which were related to his orchid and sundew research. The first one was about how plants fertilize themselves, the second about flowers that take on different forms in various circumstances, and the last was called *The Power of Movement in Plants.* All were too specialized and technical to arouse much public interest. But Darwin didn't care; he had made his mark and now he was happy to publish small volumes on whatever interested him at the moment.

In November 1877 his old school, Cambridge, awarded him an honorary doctorate. Darwin normally shrugged off such awards, but this one was special to him. Even though he had never been a very keen student, Cambridge still wanted to honor him this way. It was proof that his life's work had made an impact, and that he was respected by the highest levels of society.

The End of an Era

Darwin spent the last few years of his life studying—of all things—earthworms. He was one of the first to realize that worms are essential to life on Earth. Almost all the topsoil in the world, he discovered, is composed of the *castings* (droppings) of earthworms that chew up dead plants. Every square foot of ground, wherever he looked, had worms crawling around, chewing up and digesting whatever they came across. Billions of worms all

Cartoonists joked that Darwin was saying we are all descended from worms.

over the world chewing and digesting for millions of years had turned all the dead plants that ever grew into a layer of fertile ground that served as the foundation in which more plants could grow. Darwin saw this action as part of the grand, slow-motion changes that shaped the Earth according to his and Lyell's theories. He wanted to give earthworms their proper respect. He kept them in pots in his study and concocted all sorts of experiments to observe how they worked. He would even stand out in the rain in the middle of the night watching them crawl in and out of the ground.

He published his results in 1881, in a book called *The Formation of Vegetable Mould, Through the Action of Worms.* He made a special trip to London to convince his publisher to release it, as Darwin was sure that few people would ever buy a book on such an obscure subject. Reluctantly, the publisher agreed.

To everyone's astonishment, *Worms* became the most popular book Darwin ever wrote. The publisher could hardly print copies fast enough. Gardening was—and remains—one of the most popular hobbies in England, and thousands of gardeners were curious about what the great Charles Darwin had to say about worms and soil. Who would have suspected that worms were so important? The cartoonists leaped into action again, this time giving their satirical Darwin drawings a wormy theme.

Shortly after his worm project was completed, Darwin's heart started giving him trouble. He knew he didn't have long to live. He made out his will and told Emma he wasn't afraid of dying.

Finally, on the afternoon of April 19, 1882, Darwin's heart gave out and he died at Down House, surrounded by his family. An era had come to a close.

Emma made preparations to bury him in the village graveyard. But Darwin's scientific friends had bigger plans. They felt that in death Darwin should be given the highest honor of all. Many of the greatest men in British history were buried in London's famous Westminster Abbey, which everyone treated as a shrine to the nation's heritage.

Huxley, Hooker, and all of Darwin's influential friends agreed that Darwin should be buried here as well. Emma and the rest of the family wanted him nearby, but in the end they agreed to give Darwin to the nation, to have him interred forever in a place where all could pay their respects.

And so on April 26, 1882, Darwin was laid to rest in Westminster Abbey, just a few feet from the grave of England's other legendary scientist, Isaac Newton. *The Voyage of Charles Darwin* was finally at an end.

Or was it just beginning?

8

After Darwin

The name of Charles Darwin is now recognized all over the world, and his theory is accepted by all scientists as the foundation of biology, the study of life. But it hasn't always been this way. Though his theory of evolution was hailed during his lifetime, there was a long period between then and now when almost everyone rejected it. If it wasn't for the work of a modest and little-known monk named Gregor Mendel, Charles Darwin might have been completely forgotten.

The Problem

As far back as the 1860s, a few of Darwin's critics began to point out what seemed to be a major problem with his theory of evolution through natural selection. Even if a useful variation *did* occur in a species, they said, it would get "washed out" over many generations so that after a while it would disappear entirely. Say, for example, that a deer was born with extra strong legs that enabled it to escape from predators more successfully than its siblings could. According to Darwin, it would survive and grow up to have many baby deer (fawns) that would inherit its strong legs. But, the critics pointed out, in order to have offspring the extra-fast deer would have to mate with a normal deer (since there would be no other extra-fast deer yet), and so their fawns would have one fast parent and one normal parent. Thus it would make sense that the fawns would not be as fast as their speedy father. And when those fawns grew up they too would have normal mates, so their offspring would be even more average. After several generations, the beneficial variation of having strong legs would be overwhelmed by the averageness of

Clarence Darrow (seen here standing and facing the audience) was a brilliant speaker.

all the other deer. So, the critics claimed, it wasn't really possible for natural selection to lead to any new features at all, much less a new species.

Darwin could never find a good answer to this question. Nor could anyone else at the time; well into the 20th century, this problem of "blended inheritance" stumped all the leading scientists. But the answer was right under their noses.

Gregor Mendel

In the town of Brünn in what was then the country of Austria-Hungary (now the town is called Brno and it's in the Czech Republic), a mild-mannered monk named Gregor Mendel decided to perform some interesting experiments in his spare time. Mendel did not know Darwin and was completely unaware of the excitement over evolution that was sweeping England. But he happened to be solving the biggest problem of Darwin's theory.

Between 1857 and 1865, Mendel grew special varieties of pea plants in the monastery garden. He was trying to figure out the nature of heritability: how and why do offspring look like their parents? He chose pea plants because they had several types of features that could be easily measured. Some made green seeds, some made yellow; some were tall plants, some were short; and so on. Mendel fertilized yellow pea plants with pollen from green pea plants. After the seeds matured, he opened the pods and found they were all yellow. They were *not* greenish yellow, but pure yellow; the traits of the

parents had not blended in the offspring. That was strange, but things soon got stranger. He allowed these second-generation yellow peas to self-fertilize, and when he opened the resulting third-generation pods a while later he found that three-fourths of the peas were yellow but one-fourth were green! The green trait had somehow remained hidden in the yellow peas and reappeared in later generations.

Mendel spent eight years performing all sorts of experiments like this, and keeping careful records the whole time. In the end he reached several important conclusions:

- Every organism inherits traits from its parents.
- Each parent contributes exactly half of these "inheritance factors" (which are now called *genes*).
- If the two parents have different traits, usually these traits will *not* "blend" in the offspring; one feature will show itself (be "dominant"), and the other will remain hidden (be "recessive").
- The hidden "recessive" gene will not disappear; if two parents with the same recessive gene have offspring, the hidden trait can re-emerge.

Say, for example, that your father's father was very tall, but his wife (your grandmother) was very short. When they had your father, it turned out that he was short like his mother. The same thing happened on the other side of your family: a tall man and a short woman had a short daughter (your mother). Then your parents got together and had you and your siblings. Since both your parents are

Gregor Mendel.

This picture shows Mendel's pea plants growing in the monastery garden.

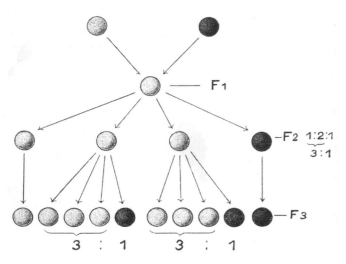

A yellow pea and a green pea will combine to produce a first-generation (F1) offspring that is yellow. But that new yellow pea will produce one green pea (F2) for every three yellow offspring. Later generations will follow strict genetic patterns.

short, will you be short too? Not necessarily! Both your father and your mother may have hidden recessive tall genes, which they would have inherited from your grandfathers. In this particular example, Mendel proved that you would have a one in four chance of being tall even if both your parents are short.

Mendel used precise mathematics to show that many features of the pea plants followed the same predictable pattern. He published his results in a German-language journal with a very small circulation. Few people read it, and it was quickly forgotten. Mendel was disappointed but he was soon thereafter promoted to run the whole monastery anyway, and for the rest of his life he no longer had free time to be a scientist.

The Rediscovery

Many years later, in 1900, another scientist found a copy of Mendel's paper. He was amazed! This unknown monk had made an important discovery about inheritance that no one had noticed.

News about Mendel's research spread throughout Europe, and people started performing similar experiments with other plants and animals to confirm his results. They found that the same inheritance patterns applied to *all* organisms, not just pea plants. Furthermore, they discovered that certain traits *do* blend, but even so, Mendel's principles of dominant and recessive genes were still true. In the illustration, for example, a black chicken and a white

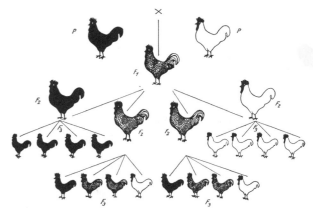

The genetic patterns for chickens (and other species) are exactly the same as for peas. Gray chickens still hold pure black genes and pure white genes, which appear in their offspring.

rooster will produce a gray chicken, but that gray chicken will produce offspring that will be either gray, black, or white. The crucial thing to remember is that the genes for black or white feathers do not disappear or become permanently blended together.

For a long time no one saw any connection between these genetic experiments and Darwin's theory of evolution. Natural selection was still out of favor because no one had ever found an answer to the critics who said that beneficial traits would average out and thus vanish over time.

Genetics and the Modern Synthesis

Starting in the 1920s, however, scientists began to realize how "Mendelian" genetics solved the problems facing Darwin's theory of evolution. Mendel's experiments showed that the critics of natural selection had been mistaken. Beneficial variations would *not* get washed out and disappear. If a new trait was from a dominant gene, one parent would pass it on to offspring unchanged. This meant that beneficial new features that aided survival and reproduction could spread throughout a whole species. Even a recessive gene would spread, though more slowly. Natural selection could work after all! Darwin's reputation was saved.

The combination of Darwinian evolution and Mendelian genetics was given a new name: the Modern Synthesis. *Synthesis* means combining two or more ideas into one new idea. It's also sometimes called *Neo-Darwinism* (*neo-* means new). The Modern Synthesis is the theory of evolution that all scientists accept today. It brings together all the best ideas about evolution, old and new, into one grand theory that explains all the evidence discovered since Darwin's time.

The Modern Synthesis is not one single theory that can be described in a few words. But here are some of its basic ideas:

- Evolution has occurred throughout history and continues to occur.
- Causes of evolution include both natural selection and *genetic drift* (explained below).
- The information describing every feature of an organism is contained in tiny particles called genes, which are passed on from parent to offspring through reproduction.
- Variations in organisms are caused by unique

combinations of parental genes, and also by small genetic mutations, which can make the organism inheriting them have a slightly new and different physical form.

- Only certain genes determine an individual's appearance; other genes are not "expressed" and are passed on from generation to generation until, according to Mendel's laws, they may manifest themselves under certain circumstances.
- Evolution occurs in small steps, little by little, as Darwin insisted.

Genetic drift means that some traits may arise at random that are neither helpful nor harmful to an organism's chances for survival. New genes may also appear that have no effect on an organism's form. Once they appear, these traits and genes can spread throughout the population, even though they serve no purpose. The word "drift" refers to any sort of random or accidental evolutionary change that is not caused or affected by natural selection.

The Discovery of DNA

There was still one problem with genetics and the Modern Synthesis: no one had ever seen a gene! Mendel proved that they existed, but no one knew what they looked like or how they worked on a microscopic level. Between the 1920s and the 1940s, scientists looked deeper and deeper into cells with more and more powerful instruments. They discovered chromosomes, which looked like tiny strings, inside every cell of the body. Experiments showed that chromosomes contained the genes, but the genes were still too small to be seen.

It was not until 1953 that the secret was finally unlocked. As the result of the work of many scientists, a molecule inside the chromosomes was discovered to be the actual carrier of genetic information. This molecule was called DNA, which is an abbreviation for its official chemical name, **d**eoxyribo**n**ucleic **a**cid. The DNA molecule was very long and looked like two interlocked springs, a shape called a *double helix*. Genes, it turned out, were segments along this long molecule. Each segment controlled a different aspect of the genetic code. It wasn't until 2001 when scientists finally figured out which segments contained which genes for human beings. It took almost 150 years to complete Mendel's research.

The Evolution of Evolution

In the century and a half since Darwin's time, experts in almost every field have come to adopt his theory of evolution. Astronomers see evolution at work in the formation of stars and galaxies and in the history of the universe. Psychologists now speculate that many human emotions and ways of thinking are the result of natural selection. Economists, philosophers, anthropologists, and others are all beginning to see that evolution through natural selection has significance far beyond the realm of plants and animals. A good example can be found in the field of linguistics, which is the study of languages and words.

Linguists today use the theory of evolution to trace how languages change through time. They realize that the same principle of natural selection that Darwin applied to animals also applies to *words*. If a word is no longer useful in a language, people will stop saying it and it will slowly disappear. The word *couter,* for example, used to mean the part of a suit of armor that covers the elbow. But hardly anyone wears armor anymore, so no one has a reason to talk about couters these days. The word no longer had a purpose in the language and, as it fell into disuse, natural selection has eliminated it.

On the other hand, new words appear to describe new aspects of society. Thirty years ago nobody sent electronic messages to each other on their computers. Hence, there was no word in our language to describe such an activity. But once it became possible to send messages this way, the language needed a new word to communicate the concept: *e-mail.* The more popular sending messages electronically became, the more people had a reason to talk about it. After a while, e-mail became one of the most common words in the language.

Old words go extinct and new words emerge. This is linguistic evolution at work, as the language adapts to the changing human environment.

Social Darwinism

Social Darwinism is not a scientific theory but rather a philosophy about human society. Darwin himself did not think up Social Darwinism. In fact, he had nothing to do with it. The philosophy was merely named after him by a British writer named Herbert Spencer.

Spencer was a philosopher who lived during Darwin's time. He too was interested in evolution, but not as it related to animals and plants. Spencer was more interested in how societies and civilizations evolve. He compared human society to a natural environment. Just as species and ecosystems evolved in nature, he wrote, civilizations and countries evolve as well. Spencer felt it was wrong to interfere with the natural progress of evolution, and that we should let nature take its course in human affairs as it does in the wild.

He also declared that all individuals have human rights, and that no other person and no government should be allowed to take these rights away. The guiding principle in human affairs should be freedom. Spencer proposed that the government should just leave people alone and let each person do what makes him or her happiest.

Spencer had always promoted the concept of evolution (in fact, he was one of the first people to use the word *evolution* in the way we mean it today), and when he read Darwin's *Origin of Species* he was very excited that someone had finally proven that things really do evolve. Spencer took some of Darwin's concepts about natural selection and ap-

plied them to people as well. He then came up with a new phrase to describe how Darwin's theory applied to human society: "survival of the fittest." As mentioned earlier, this motto was so catchy that everyone started using it, even Darwin himself. Spencer had so much respect for Darwin that he later named his philosophy "Social Darwinism" after him. Darwin was not very happy about people using his name to describe ideas that were not his and that he did not necessarily even like. Spencer wasn't the only one to use Darwin's name; all sorts of politicians and philosophers insisted that evolution proved they were right.

In Spencer's view, "survival of the fittest," when applied to human society, meant that some people will succeed in life and become happy and wealthy, while others will fail and become miserable and poor. Those who were "fittest"—stronger, smarter, harder working, and so on—would naturally rise to the top of society. Everyone else would be eliminated, through hunger and disease. In this way human society would continually improve, he wrote, because the "best" people would survive at the expense of those "less fit."

Nowadays most people think Social Darwinism is too cruel. Human beings are not like animals, people say, and human society is not a jungle. Just because certain people *are* poor doesn't mean they *deserve* to be poor. Especially in Victorian England, a child who was born into a poor family had almost no chance of ever making a better life for him- or herself. Other writers have pointed out that many animal species have evolved to *cooperate* and help each other; often this is the best way for a

Herbert Spencer.

species to survive. Perhaps Spencer is mistaken; cooperation is as much a part of evolution as is competition.

The Battle over Evolution Today

If all scientists now accept the theory of evolution, then why is it still controversial? What are people arguing about?

The debate over evolution is different today than it was in Darwin's era. Darwin had to fight two battles at the same time: first, he had to prove that evolution really *does* happen; and next he had to prove that natural selection was the main reason evolution occurs. And he had to prove this not only to his scientific colleagues, but to the world at large.

Nowadays, the battlefield has shifted. There is no longer any doubt in the scientific community that evolution has happened and continues to happen. It has been proven countless times and is recognized as one of the basic principles of nature.

There is also universal agreement that natural selection is a cause of evolution. The only remaining argument among scientists is *how much* natural selection affects evolution. Is it the *only* cause, as Darwin said? Or do other effects related to genetics also play a role? Arguments like this are common among scientists in all fields. It is, in fact, how science works; people debate different positions until everyone finally agrees that one side is right or wrong.

But there are a few misinformed nonscientists who still insist that evolution does not exist at all. Almost all these people think that the Bible is always true, and that evolution contradicts the Bible. Thus, they say, evolution is false. This was the same argument that people used against evolution during Darwin's time. Because these people believe that all creatures were made directly by God during the creation as described in Genesis, they are now called *creationists*.

When creationists try to prove their point, they often say, "Look, the scientists themselves are still arguing over evolution! If they can't agree, then how can the rest of us be expected to believe that evolution exists? The matter has still not been settled, so it's better to play it safe and not assume that evolution is real."

At first glance it looks as if they have a point. It's true, of course, that scientists still debate evolution. But they're *not* debating whether or not it exists. As mentioned above, scientists agree that evolution is real; they're merely debating the details of how it works. Yet most people don't follow the specifics of what scientists are arguing about. They only know the scientists are arguing about *something.* So the creationists' claim that evolution is *not* an accepted scientific fact is still believed by many people around the world.

Evolution in the Schools?

Most of the current fight between creationists and scientists has to do with whether evolution should be taught in school. The creationists claim that evolution has never been proven, so it should be kept out of the classroom. Scientists naturally claim the opposite: evolution is as true as any other scientific theory and should be part of every child's education.

In most states evolution is treated no differently than any other aspect of science. Teachers are free to teach evolution if they want to. But not in every state. A few states, including Kansas, Alabama, and Arkansas, have recently passed laws or guidelines restricting the teaching of evolution, and allowing creationism to be taught in some science classes. The laws are challenged, but not always successfully. Every year the struggle between science and creationism continues all over the country, and over half the states have at some time or another debated whether or not to teach evolution.

The Scopes Trial

The debate over evolution in American schools got its start in 1925 in one of history's most famous trials. William Jennings Bryan, a former presidential candidate and Christian Fundamentalist preacher, had for years been demanding that evolution be banned from American schools. Bryan was so popular and persuasive that several states began to follow his advice. In 1925 Tennessee became the first state to make it a crime for any teacher to tell his or her students about evolution.

The law was welcomed in Tennessee, but many people in the rest of the country were outraged. Free-speech advocates wanted to overturn the law, but to do so they had to find someone willing to be accused of teaching evolution. That way, the law could be fought in court. They found their volunteer in a young high school football coach named John Scopes, who had taught a few science classes as a substitute teacher in the Dayton, Tennessee, high school. It hadn't been Scopes's idea to teach evolution—it was still part of the statewide science textbook that every teacher had to use. He "confessed" to teaching evolution and was charged with breaking the law.

Forces on both sides of the debate saw this as a chance to prove a point. The prosecution, which wanted to find Scopes guilty and keep evolution illegal, brought in the best lawyers they could find, including William Jennings Bryan himself. Scopes's defense team included the top free-speech attorneys from all over the country, including a famous and controversial attorney named Clarence Darrow. Darrow was notorious for taking on the most scandalous and shocking cases. He was considered the most effective lawyer in the country.

Just as in Darwin's day, newspapers and magazines saw the trial as an opportunity to stir up emotions and poke fun at the notion that humans are related to monkeys. For weeks the trial was front-page news all over the country. It was the first news event ever to be broadcast live on the radio. All of

William Jennings Bryan fanning himself in the hot courtroom.

John Scopes.

Though this chimpanzee was never allowed to testify at the trial, he entertained curiosity-seekers in Dayton every day.

America was fascinated by the case, which became known as the "Monkey Trial."

In truth, no one really cared whether Scopes was innocent or guilty, or if the law violated the U.S. Constitution. The trial was seen as a battle between conservative, old-fashioned Christian values and modern intellectual freedom. Darrow even said, "Scopes isn't on trial. *Civilization* is on trial."

Who would prevail?

The small town of Dayton became like a carnival. Reporters, preachers, and curiosity-seekers flocked there to witness history in the making. Someone even brought a chimpanzee to testify in the trial; the chimp quickly became the most popular attraction in town.

Every day, over a thousand spectators crowded into the hot courtroom during the summer of 1925.

The defense first tried to argue that the case should be thrown out because the law was unconstitutional. The judge, who was a fan of Bryan's, denied the motion. After a few witnesses testified that Scopes had indeed taught evolution to his class, the defense tried to bring in expert scientists as witnesses. But after the first expert, a zoologist who discussed mankind's relationship to other species, the judge forbade any more scientific testimony. The case isn't about whether evolution is true, he argued, but only about whether Mr. Scopes broke the law.

It was so crowded in the courtroom that the floor was about to collapse, and it was much too hot as well. The judge moved the trial outside onto the courthouse lawn. Now 5,000 spectators gathered to watch. Since Darrow was not allowed to discuss evolution at the trial, he decided he would call witnesses to discuss the Bible instead. His first surprise witness: William Jennings Bryan himself! Even though he was on the opposing team, he *was* an expert on the Bible. Thinking it was a great chance to show off his knowledge and expertise, Bryan agreed. But Darrow had led him into a trap. Darrow knew that the Bible contradicted itself in parts and that it was impossible to prove in a court of law that the Bible was always literally true. Before long, Darrow's questions had Bryan's logic going in circles. The audience for the first time started to laugh at Bryan. The judge suddenly brought an end to the questioning.

But it was all just for show. None of this did anything to prove that Scopes was innocent of breaking the law. The jury quickly found him guilty, and the judge fined him $100. Technically, Darrow had lost, but the reporters (who were mostly

The Great "Monkey Trial" Debate

The 1925 trial of Tennessee teacher John Scopes, charged with the "crime" of telling his students about Darwin, was the first time evolution was ever debated in court. Scopes was found guilty, but many people feel that the trial was a victory for evolution anyway because of the great arguments presented by defense attorney Clarence Darrow. In this activity you'll reenact the trial: which side will win this time?

What you need
At least two friends or relatives (the more the better)

Choose one person to be William Jennings Bryan (who will argue *against* evolution), and one person to be Clarence Darrow (who will argue *for* evolution). If you can't choose, flip a coin to decide. The third person will take the role of the judge. Any other people will act as the jury.

Before the mock trial begins, the people playing Bryan and Darrow should write down the arguments they plan to use. (Make use of all the knowledge you've learned in this book.) Here are a few good ones to get you started:

Debate Points for William Jennings Bryan

- Scientists still argue about evolution, so how do we know it's true if even the experts disagree?
- The people of Tennessee have the right to teach their kids whatever they want.
- Evolution is just a theory, not a fact.
- Darwin didn't know all the answers. He had mistaken notions about heredity and other important topics. If his other ideas were wrong, how can we be so sure that his one famous idea—evolution—is right?
- John Scopes himself admits that he is guilty as charged. There's nothing to argue about.
- If we admit that we are descended from monkeys, then people will think they can act like animals, and civilization itself will collapse.

Debate Points for Clarence Darrow

- Two hundreds years' worth of scientific observations and experiments have proven beyond the slightest doubt that evolution exists.
- The law is unconstitutional because it forces people to accept one religious viewpoint. The Constitution says that the government cannot promote any religion.
- Just because evolution is outlawed in Tennessee doesn't make it untrue. The rest of the world still accepts evolution. And the rest of the world will laugh at students from Tennessee for not knowing what everyone else knows.
- We can't base our legal system on the Bible because the Bible is full of all sorts of strange ideas and contradictions that make no sense in the modern world.
- It doesn't matter whether Darwin himself was right or wrong or had all the answers. Many scientists since Darwin's time have shown that evolution is as real as you and me.
- I'm not here to say John Scopes is innocent of breaking the law. I'm here to say that the law itself is a crime against everything America stands for.

If you can think of better arguments, write those down too. When everyone's ready, the judge should announce that the court is in session. Each side then should take turns presenting one argument at a time. The prosecution (Bryan) should go first and make a statement that lasts no more than two or three minutes. Then the defense has a turn to "rebut" (argue against) the prosecution's statement, and to make a statement of his or her own. And so on, back and forth. Neither side has the right to interrupt the other. The judge should keep order in the court, limit each statement to three minutes at most, and not take sides.

After both sides have given all their arguments, the judge (or jury, if you have one) will decide who is the winner.

After the trial, rent or check out from the library a tape of the film *Inherit the Wind*. Watch it with your parents. Although many names and historical details were changed, the film is based on the Scopes trial and gives a good idea of how the *real* Darrow and Bryan debated.

pro-evolution) declared that Bryan had been humiliated and that the case had really been a great victory for the cause of evolution.

Shortly after the trial was over, Bryan died in his sleep, Darrow retired, and John Scopes secretly confessed to a reporter that he never *had* taught evolution—he had accidentally skipped that lesson!

Evolution: The Next Step

Where does the story of evolution go from here? Scientists from many fields continue to study evolution and its effects every day.

In Darwin's era there were almost no fossils related to the evolution of the human race. He had to speculate that humans were related to apes based on indirect evidence. Now, however, scientists have

the direct evidence that Darwin lacked. In the last 50 years anthropologists have discovered thousands of "missing link" fossils. They show that *homo sapiens* evolved in eastern Africa sometime between 200,000 and one million years ago. Fossils going back even further show that humans did indeed once have ancestors that were apelike. Sophisticated modern analysis of DNA has shown that humankind is very closely related to chimpanzees and gorillas, just as Darwin and Huxley had suspected and as the Victorians had feared.

The Future Evolution of the Human Race

But what about human beings? What does the future hold for us? Will we continue to evolve,

Future Evolution

How will humans evolve in the future? What features will be useful to us thousands of centuries from now? Can you predict what humans will look like after a million more years of evolution?

What you need
drawing pad or blank sheets of paper
colored pens, pencils, or crayons

Will humans evolve to acquire any of these traits?
fur (to survive the next ice age)
gills (to breathe underwater when the Earth floods)
a giant skull (to hold our powerful brains)
extra arms (to do more work)

eyes in the back of our heads
wings
huge muscles

Can you think of other traits that might help us survive in a million years? What will be our future environment: Outer space? Underwater? Crowded cities? A ruined Earth? Other planets? How will our new traits help us in these new environments? Will we evolve tiny bodies? Will our bodies and minds stay the same while we merely change the way we live? Or will we have no bodies at all? Could humans become nothing more than digital information in a computer?

Draw a picture of the way you think humans are *likely* to become, considering environmental changes (wings and extra limbs, for example, are extremely unlikely, considering our current anatomy). Next, draw some pictures of the way you *wish* people would look many years from now.

or have we stopped evolving altogether?

Many modern philosophers think that humankind has changed the rules for our own evolution forever. Unlike all other species, we can alter our environment to our liking. We no longer have to adapt to changing conditions—we make the conditions adapt to us. We've created a social environment where the concept "survival of the fittest" no longer applies. Nowadays, how strong or smart you are has little or no effect on whether or not you'll grow up to pass your genes onto your children. Natural selection only happens in nature, and we no longer live in nature.

This has led some people to predict a different fate for the human race: *devolution* (from *de-*, meaning the reverse of, + evolution). The theory of devolution states that we will devolve into a *less fit* species in the future. Why?

Long ago, if someone had a genetic disorder or was born with a severe handicap of some kind, odds are they wouldn't survive very long, and if they did they probably wouldn't have any children. But amazing medical advances can now help people with all sorts of disabilities to grow up and live normal lives. So their genes are passed on to their children, who may inherit the same traits. It's no longer true that only the "fittest" survive; now everybody can survive. Will genetic disorders and severe handicaps become more and more common?

Luckily, there's no real evidence that humans are devolving. That idea is still just speculation. Most scientists and thinkers aren't so pessimistic. They see a bright future ahead for human beings. As a species we've become so intelligent that we can shape our world to make it a better place. And one day we may be able to shape *ourselves* into something better as well.

The theory of evolution is still going strong. Every day we learn more about it. Evolution itself is evolving! If only Darwin were here to see it happen.

Glossary

ACQUIRED CHARACTERISTICS: features and attributes that animals and people accumulate throughout their lives, as opposed to features they are born with. Examples of *acquired characteristics* include scars, strong muscles, knowledge, or broken bones.

ADAPTATION: the process of a species changing its features over time to fit into its environment.

BARNACLE: a type of small crustacean that lives in the ocean and attaches itself to rocks, ships, or other large objects. Darwin spent years studying barnacles.

BOTANY: the scientific study of plants.

CREATIONISM: the belief that stories in the Bible are literally true as historical and scientific facts; specifically, the belief that 6,000 years ago God created the universe, the earth and all life (including humans) in only six days, as described in the Book of Genesis.

DNA: a type of molecule found in the cells of every living organism that contains all the genetic information needed to control heredity; DNA is short for deoxyribonucleic acid.

ENVIRONMENT: the natural setting in which an animal or plant lives. Climate, soil type, nearby animals and plants, terrain, and other factors make up each kind of environment.

EVOLUTION: the tendency of all species to slowly change with each passing generation as an adaptation to the surrounding environment. *Evolution* also means any kind of gradual progression or change.

EXTINCT: having no examples left alive. When the last member of an animal or plant species dies, that species goes *extinct*.

FOSSIL: the preserved remains of an animal or plant that have turned to stone after being buried for thousands or millions of years.

GALAPAGOS: a small group of rocky islands off the coast of Ecuador, which Darwin visited in 1835.

GENETICS: the study of the inheritance of features that are transmitted from parents to offspring through microscopic particles called genes.

GEOLOGY: the study of the Earth and its natural history, as revealed in its rocks, soil, and other features.

HEREDITY: the passing of physical traits from one generation to the next. Children look like their parents because of *heredity*.

MIMICRY: the natural ability of certain plants and animals to precisely imitate the appearance of other plants or animals for purposes of camouflage or deception.

NATURAL HISTORY: the study of anything to do with nature, living organisms, or the Earth. Zoology (the study of animals), vulcanology (the study of volcanoes), and meteorology (the study of the weather) are some of the many aspects of natural history.

NATURAL SELECTION: part of Darwin's theory of evolution stating that those organisms that are best adapted to any environment tend to survive and have more offspring than less well-adapted organisms. As a result, nature seems to "select" those features that benefit survival, because the offspring inherit them from their successful parents.

ORGANISM: any kind of individual living thing. Each separate animal, plant, or bacterium is an *organism*.

PALEONTOLOGY: the study of extinct plants and animals—such as dinosaurs—by looking at their fossils and other ancient remains.

SCIENCE: the accumulated knowledge of humankind describing how the physical world works, based on observable facts and theories that best explain those facts.

SEXUAL SELECTION: an aspect of natural selection explaining that some animals acquire features that serve no function other than to attract mates. Male peacocks evolved beautiful tail feathers, for example, because long-ago female peahens preferred to mate with those early peacocks that had the prettiest feathers.

SOCIAL DARWINISM: a controversial philosophy stating that the "survival of the fittest" applies to human beings (not just animals), and that successful, rich, and powerful people dominate society because of their natural abilities. Darwin himself did not invent Social Darwinism; it was merely named after him by others.

SPECIES: any specific category of animals that has evolved to be distinctly different from all other animals. Each member of a species closely resembles its fellow members in most physical attributes.

STRATA: layers of soil or rock in the Earth's crust that indicate geologic changes throughout time. (The singular of strata is *stratum*.)

TAXONOMY: the classification of animals and plants into different categories—such as genus, order, and species—according to their physical features.

THEORY: a general scientific principle formulated to explain proven facts and observations. Theories often change as more facts are discovered.

TRANSITIONAL FORMS: fossils that appear to be the remains of animals that are "in-between" existing types found today and earlier types that preceded them. The existence of *transitional forms* proves that animals can evolve from one species into another.

TRANSMUTATION: the changing from one form into another. Darwin used the term *transmutation of species* to describe the slow process of evolution.

VARIATION: a range of minor differences between members of the same species. Since no two animals are exactly alike, the aspects of each animal that differ from similar animals are called *variations*.

Resources

WEB SITES FOR FURTHER EXPLORATION

The About Darwin page

http://www.aboutdarwin.com/index.html

Facts and details about every aspect of Charles
Darwin's life, with many interesting pictures you
won't find anywhere else.

The BBC Evolution Web site

http://www.bbc.co.uk/education/darwin/index.shtml

Has an online evolution game, the complete text of *On
the Origin of Species,* a special section about
extinctions, and much more.

The PBS Evolution page

http://www.pbs.org/wgbh/evolution/

A Web site exploring all aspects of evolution and Darwin's
life, with many beautiful pictures and film clips. Part
of the popular public television "Evolution" series.

Galapagos Research Station home page

http://www.darwinfoundation.org/

Take a virtual visit to the Galapagos islands and find out
what scientists are discovering there right now!

Down House page

http://www.williamcalvin.com/bookshelf/down_hse.htm

A Web site that shows what Darwin's longtime home
Down House looks like today. The building is now
open to the public, and this site includes
information on how to visit it.

The Scopes Trial page

http://www.law.umkc.edu/faculty/projects/ftrials/
scopes/scopes.htm

Everything you ever wanted to know about the famous
"Monkey Trial" of John Scopes; you can even see
rare film footage actually taken during the trial.

How to find thousands more pages

http://www.google.com/advanced_search

There are thousands of Web sites about Darwin and
evolution, many of them quite interesting. On this
Web page, type in what you want to find—
"Galapagos," or "dinosaur fossils," for example—and
it will show you almost every Web site ever created
on that topic!

**SELECTED BIBLIOGRAPHY AND FURTHER
READING**

Appleman, Philip. *Darwin.* New York: Norton, 2001.

Barrett, Paul H. *The Collected Papers of Charles
Darwin: 2 Volumes.* Chicago: University of Chicago
Press, 1977.

Barrett, Paul H., and R. B. Freeman (editors). *The Works
of Charles Darwin, Vol. 10: The Foundations of the
Origin of Species: Two Essays Written in 1842 and
1844.* New York City: New York University Press, 1987.

Bowlby, John. *Charles Darwin: A New Life.* New York:
W. W. Norton, 1991.

Bowler, Peter. *Charles Darwin: The Man and His
Influence.* Oxford: Blackwell Publishers, 1990.

Bowler, Peter. *Evolution: The History of an Idea.*
California: University of California Press, 1989.

Browne, Janet. *Charles Darwin: The Power of Place.*
New York: Knopf, 2002.

Browne, Janet. *Charles Darwin: Voyaging.* New York:
Knopf, 1995.

Darwin, Charles, and Nora Barlow (editor). *The
Autobiography of Charles Darwin 1809–1882.* New
York: W. W. Norton & Company, 1993.

Darwin, Charles, et al. *The Descent of Man, and
Selection in Relation to Sex.* Princeton: Princeton
University Press, 1981.

Darwin, Charles, and Paul Ekman (editor). *The
Expression of the Emotions in Man and Animals.*
Oxford: Oxford University Press, 1998.

Darwin, Charles. *Journal of Researches into the Natural
History and Geology of the Countries Visited
During the Voyage of H.M.S. Beagle.* New York City:
AMS Press, 1972.

Darwin, Charles, and Ernst Mayr (introduction). *On the
Origin of Species: A Facsimile of the First Edition.*
Cambridge, MA: Harvard University Press, 1964.

Darwin, Charles, and Nora Barlow (editor). *Works of
Charles Darwin, Vol. 1: Diary of the Voyage of H.M.S.
Beagle.* New York City: New York University Press, 1987.

Desmond, Adrian, and James Moore. *Darwin, The Life
of a Tormented Evolutionist.* New York: W. W.
Norton & Company Inc., 1991.

Hull, D. L. *Darwin and His Critics: The Reception of
Darwin's Theory of Evolution by the Scientific
Community.* Chicago: University of Chicago Press,
1973.

Manier, Edward. *The Young Darwin and His Cultural
Circle.* Boston: D. Reidel, 1978.

Mayr, Ernst. *One Long Argument: Charles Darwin and
the Genesis of Modern Evolutionary Thought.*
Cambridge, MA: Harvard University Press, 1993.

Ruse, Michael (editor). *But Is It Science: The
Philosophical Question in the Creation/Evolution
Controversy.* Amherst, NY: Prometheus Books, 1996.

Ruse, Michael. *The Evolution Wars: A Guide to the
Debates.* Santa Barbara, CA: ABC-CLIO Inc., 2000.

Vorzimmer, Peter J. *Charles Darwin: The Years of
Controversy, the Origin of Species and Its Critics
1859–1882.* Philadelphia, PA: Temple University
Press, 1970.

Index